The Ultimate Gold Guide

The Promise, Allure, and Dangers of Today's Market for Gold

Nancy H. Rosenberg

About *The Ultimate Gold Guide*

"This is a must-read for anyone who wants to know more about the market for gold from an unbiased source. This book shares the history of gold in the world's monetary system and makes complicated economics simple – good for experienced and inexperienced investors alike."

-- Sandy Steele, marketing director for a Fortune 500 company

"I didn't know much about investing in gold before I picked up this book, but now I feel confident that I know what to look for in a market that can be intimidating."

-- Janet Civitelli, author and LPC

"*The Ultimate Gold Guide* is a must-read for everyone who is considering investing in gold."

-- Mark Bowles, commercial insurance agent and investor

ISBN: 9781470025274

www.TheUltimateGoldGuide.com

Other books by Nancy H. Rosenberg:

Outwitting Stress—A Practical Guide
To Conquering Stress Before You Crack

Outwitting Housework—Brilliant Tips,
Tricks, and Advice on Housekeeping…
and Life

Off Your Rocker! The Ultimate Guide
for Grandparents *(with Judy Haire)*

Waking in a Wide Land
A Novel

Table of Contents

Author's Note

I am not an economist. I don't have any vested interest in whether or not you buy or sell gold. I'm a writer, I'm good at researching, and I'm curious. My career as a writer has revolved around finding topics I want to know more about, then digging in to learn more. I worked as an editor for the Central Intelligence Agency, wrote a book about stress management, and have had articles appear in a wide variety of publications, including *Woman's Day*, *Fitness*, *Cigar Aficionado*, and *U.S. Airways' Attache*.

This book began with a question, "What's the deal with all these ads for gold?" They seem to be everywhere: on the radio, banner ads on the Internet, full-page ads in the newspaper. These ubiquitous ads, along with "We Buy Gold!" storefronts sprouting like mushrooms, made me wonder what all the fuss was about.

It wasn't just the sheer number of ads. After all, there are lots of ads out there, for everything from pharmaceuticals to jewelry. There was something about these particular ads for gold that struck me as predatory. They seem to be very subtly stoking and then appealing to fear.

Then I started to notice the ads that made selling scrap gold so easy, "You don't even have to leave your house! Just mail us your gold and we'll send you a check!" That was it. For me, the hand of the marketers was tipped. The overt appeal to the housebound--possibly elderly, probably prone to suggestions of systemic economic collapse--was too much.

I determined to find out as much as I could about the market for gold, and to make it widely available to anyone who wants to know more, in a condensed form, from an unbiased source. I wanted to know the truth. For the average person, is gold a good investment? Why or why not?

I dug in. For over a year, I read every article I could find about gold. I watched the market rise and fall, studied its history, and learned to view the market not as a mysterious, unknowable cache of potential wealth, but as a commodity with its own variables. I also learned that, true to my suspicions, it is a minefield of unscrupulous marketers and opportunists.

For me, assembling this information has been an education. I hope you read it and feel the same.

-- *Nancy Rosenberg*

Introduction

You've seen the ads. You've heard the commercials. The sales pitches are shrill: "Buy gold NOW!" Sometimes there's an implied threat: "Before it's *too late!*"

As with any hard sell, those making the pitch have an aura about them of absolute certainty.

What's the story there? Why the hard sell? And why the scare tactics?

It is a fundamental of commodities trading that at every price point, someone is betting that the cost will go up. Those are the buyers. Sellers assume or predict or hope that the price will go down. They are hoping to make money while the price is still high.

Keep this in mind as we explore the history and the current trends in the volatile, unpredictable, somewhat mystical world of buying and selling gold.

There's another layer to the hard sell that is characterized by personalities using the weight of their reputation to sell gold. Glenn Beck hawks for Goldline International. So do Alan Colmes and Sean Hannity. Pat Boone receives a commission for advertising gold. So do Laura Ingraham, Mike Huckabee, and Fred Thompson.

You may notice that, in many cases, those touting gold also mention the virtual certainty of calamitous times ahead. They use terms like "currency devaluation," "runaway inflation," and "digital money," and they can be masters of instilling fear. They tout gold not so much as a wise investment, but as a sort of insurance policy against global financial collapse and chaos.

Gold can and probably be should a part of any well-diversified portfolio. But, as we will see, there are smart ways to buy (and sell) gold, then there are naïve ways that will leave you short-changed and ripped off.

Fareed Zakaria, in discussing the motivations behind investing in gold, says this: "Gold isn't a stock with real earnings. It isn't a bond with interest payments. It isn't oil. It won't help you drive a car; it won't help you light a fire. Yes, you can wear it, but you can't eat it. If doomsday arrives, a can of baked beans might be worth a lot more than a brick of gold."

Finally, when examining the current market for gold, knowing a bit about the history of the metal and its allure is instructive.

The California Gold Rush happened in the years around 1850. Fifty years later, another gold rush began when a few prospectors returned from the Yukon, a dangerous, harsh northern territory that is far into the frozen tundra of Alaska. They were carrying bags of gold, and the rush was on.

Prospectors scrambled to the Yukon; a few found gold, and many died trying. But far and away the people who made the most money were those who sold pack animals, supplies, and guides to the frenzied prospectors. There was no need to risk their own personal comfort and safety when there was money to be made off the gullibility of others.

The parallels to today's market for gold are strikingly similar.

Gold has held an historical allure since the beginning of recorded history. People are willing to go to great lengths in order to obtain what they see as financial security, and gold can seem like a very safe bet. The allure of gold can defy common sense, and, in many cases, it appeals to unsophisticated investors who are driven by fear. Like the prospectors before them, many today are willing to invest in something they know little about, and the results can be dire.

The market for gold can be vicious and slick; it is filled with fear-based marketing campaigns. What is needed is an honest examination of the history and the current market for gold. If you know what gold has done in the past, then you'll know that it is not a sure-fire hedge against uncertainty. The inherent value of gold is like any other commodity: it's worth what people are willing to pay for it. If runaway inflation arrives, gold will probably be very useful. But if you buy gold from an unscrupulous seller, then you more than likely will fail to see any kind of meaningful return on your investment. Premiums, insurance, and storage fees can eat into the value of a gold investment very quickly. In short, gold can be a good hedge against inflation and currency devaluation, but it should only be a part of a diversified portfolio, and it should be purchased carefully, by investors who know something about the market and what they are buying.

Chapter 1: Delving into the Murky World of Gold

Just before 9/11, the price of an ounce of gold was $279.

Ten years later, the price of that same ounce soared past the $1,900 mark, for an increase of over 600 percent. Was it a bubble, or was it an accurate indicator of uncertain times?

What happened?

Fear is what happened. Uncertainty. The economic pandemonium of 2008 gave way to a firmly entrenched recession. And whenever people don't trust banks, don't trust the stock market, and don't trust the dollar, they turn to gold. (When trust in the dollar returns, as we've seen during the euro zone crisis, gold tends to fall correspondingly.)

The forms of gold are many and varied: coins, bars, bullion. The American Gold Eagle, South African Krugerrand, Austrian Philharmonic, Canadian Gold Maple Leaf, and the Chinese

Gold Panda are striking in their tangible value and shiny allure. They are appealing on a primal level. They speak with a silent reassurance that when (not if) other forms of currency become worthless, those who own gold will be vindicated by their wisdom and astute financial foresight.

For those recently tuning in, the case that is made for investing in gold can be compelling, but, like a shiny counterfeit, a deeper look into the business end of the gold-selling machinery reveals an industry that actively works to instill fear and then exploit it for profit.

Ads for gold rely upon a few tricks, including the ever-present chart that shows gold prices staggering up, and up, and up. The graph is a bit misleading. When you back up and incorporate longer periods of time, the upward staggering is revealed to be a relatively short-term trend. For decades, excepting a sharp increase in the early1980s, the price of gold tootled along, rising and falling with a ho-hum predictability, never rising or falling to a degree that would cause either alarm or undue cheer. What you see when you look at a long-term chart is a steady trend followed by about a decade of upward growth. In short, you see what is, in all probability, a bubble.

This is not to say that gold should not be considered as an investment. Gold has intrinsic value and can serve as a hedge against rapid changes in the currency markets. But gold is often marketed, instead, as a precious commodity that is "virtually guaranteed" to continue increasing in value.

This is simply not true. The price of gold rises and falls, just like any other commodity. Gold may rise for one year or 10, but, at some point, it is likely to fall as well.

Despite its risk, there are plenty of astute investors who are heavily invested in gold. The University of Texas endowment funds holds approximately $1 billion in gold bullion. Those who are bullish on gold are betting that the economy will stay weak, the dollar will lose value, and the U.S. Government will continue to print money to finance our debt, which will result in inflation. The weakening dollar will result in gold prices continuing to rise.

The flipside? "If our economy regains its footing and the politicians seriously start to deal with the national debt, gold prices will collapse, because the dollar will strengthen," says economist Will Deener.

A Brief but Relevant History

In many respects, the rush to buy gold is eerily reminiscent of the California Gold Rush of 1849, when prospectors from around the world heard the news that untapped veins of gold were plentiful. Hundreds of thousands poured into undeveloped wilderness. While a few got lucky, most of the easily obtained gold was quickly discovered, and heavier equipment was needed to access the rest. Individual prospectors were soon shut out by large-scale mining companies, and most of those who got rich did so by selling overpriced equipment to hungry, hopeful immigrants.

About 50 years later, the Klondike Gold Rush in Western Canada began when miners from the Yukon returned to Seattle and San

Francisco with bags of gold. The press was alerted, and the rush was on.

The Klondike Gold Rush was harsh even by California Gold Rush standards. Approximately 100,000 "stampeders" began the trip, but only 30,000 made it. Thousands of men and animals died from a lack of provisions, got killed by Indians, got lost in the wilderness, fell off treacherous mountain paths, or froze to death. The last leg of the journey was 500 miles upstream, so prospectors were required to make their own boats. Many more perished when their hand-crafted boats broke apart in the frigid Alaskan waters. The last leg of the overland journey was so steep and icy that over 3,000 pack animals fell and died.

The easiest route, naturally, was also the most expensive. Those who could afford the fee hired a boat to carry them up to Dawson City, but most went by foot. Because the route was so long and harsh, the Northwest Mounted Police required each traveler to carry a year's supply of food before they allowed them to cross the border into Canada. Pack animals were required. Merchants in increasingly scarce towns along the way made vast sums outfitting those willing to risk everything for the allure of outrageous wealth.

Once they arrived at the gold fields of Dawson City, most found that the easily accessible gold was all but gone. A few nuggets, chips, or flakes found here and there was a teasing reminder that gold had once been there, or, for the optimists, was still there, tauntingly out of sight.

Then there was the actual work required to get the gold out of the ground, which at best was icy and semi-thawed, and at worst was frozen solid. Small patches had to be dethawed and then hacked through, a messy, painful process that chewed through gloves and left hands bloodied and frozen. Most of the gold veins were 10 feet or more below ground, and what digging could be done had to be done during the summer months. In the winter, when temperatures dropped to -60 degrees, digging became impossible.

The biggest boom to hit this part of the world was a huge bust for the miners. For the most part, the only ones to strike it rich were the merchants and profiteers who took advantage of those who hoped to get rich quick.

And this is where the similarities to the Gold Rush history of the 19th century and today's massive ads urging the immediate acquisition of gold start to become apparent.

A brief perusal on the subject of gold on the Internet turns up a flurry of confusing and somewhat contradictory sites. Some want to buy gold, some want to sell gold. Some tell you what gold is worth (literally, on the stock market). Alarmingly, some tell you what gold *will be worth.* Some sites sell coins with a lot of fancy packaging. Some will store the gold for you. Some employ an impressive array of scare tactics, while others are clearly designed to appeal to aesthetes, or collectors, or those who want to own "perfect MS70" coins which have not been circulated and are literally in mint condition. Added costs are called "premiums," which are separate from delivery fees and insurance. Prices and fees vary widely from site to site.

Two things soon become apparent:

First, *gold definitely has inherent value and is inarguably a valid hedge against market volatility and potential currency devaluation.*

Second, *it is a vehicle that is easily exploited and manipulated by those who would profit from the fear and relative ignorance of others.*

Stepping Into the Fray

The issue of gold—or, more precisely, whether or not to invest in gold—has become a parlor game for pundits. Talking heads, political scientists, economists, and media personalities have been chattering for years about investing in gold. From Glenn Beck (who turned out to be paid by Goldline International for his endless shilling) to George Soros (who sold too soon) to Warren Buffett (who has never liked gold and sees stocks as the way to go), there is no shortage of opinions and predictions.

The conversation soon takes twists and turns. Gold as an investment soon turns to talk of real or perceived political and financial instability.

Should the United States return to the gold standard? What role does the International Monetary Fund play, the Federal Reserve, and how interdependent are we in the global financial system? How does the valuation of gold affect interest rates, and how can gold be used as a hedge against inflation or deflation?

Alan Greenspan thinks one thing (at one point he advocated a return to the gold standard but later revised his views). Ben Bernanke thinks something else (that gold is a hedge against uncertainty and is thus different from other commodities). Milton Friedman had plenty of ideas (a monetarist, he thought we should sell all the gold in Fort Knox and be done with any national association with gold). The issues are complex, but they are not beyond the reach of a potential investor who is willing to read up on the subject and become educated in the areas that matter. Investors don't need to understand complex candlestick graphs or currency formulas and prognostications, but what they do need is a basic understanding of the history, emotional appeal, legitimate value, and dangers of the gold market.

Chapter 2: Gold 101

Gold, silver, platinum and palladium are the major metals in which people invest. These metals have wide uses in addition to coins and jewelry: they are also widely used in the development of computer parts, electronics, medical equipment, water purification processes, photo processing, and the refining and purification of oil and natural gas.

The element gold (Au) has several unique properties, including a malleability that can allow it to be spun into micro threads or pounded into wafer-thin sheets. It's virtually indestructible: gold can be melted and remelted without losing any of its chemical properties. It remains shiny and lustrous, it doesn't tarnish or fade, and it doesn't degrade over time.

What Is Palladium?

Palladium is one of the platinum group metals and is used extensively as a key component in the manufacturing of catalytic converters.

Palladium is also one of the three most used metals (along with nickel and silver) which can be alloyed with gold to produce "white gold."

In November 2005 the Royal Canadian Mint introduced the first palladium product, the Palladium Maple Leaf Coin. A single maple leaf appears on the reverse of this coin, which is the national symbol of Canada. A sculpture Queen Elizabeth II adorns the obverse.

What Is Platinum?

Far more rare than gold, it is estimated that all of the platinum ever mined would fit into a cube less than 25 feet on each side. More than half of all platinum is used in the automotive industry to control vehicle exhaust emissions, but it has a host of other uses, including high-end jewelry production.

So, you think you're ready to buy gold. What do you need to know?

Exchange Traded Funds

There are several ways to buy gold. You can buy actual coins, bars, or bullion, or you can buy stock in an ETF (Exchange Traded Fund). When you buy an ETF, you are typically investing in a conglomerate of companies. The fund purchases and stores the gold, and the value of the fund rises or falls based on the price of gold.

Gold ETFs provide a method for investing in gold without the logistics of insurance, storing, maintaining, testing, moving, or reselling. With a gold ETF, trading in gold can be done very easily, at any time during market hours, using an online brokerage account. Investing in gold ETFs also allows for more incremental investments: you can buy in portions of an ounce.

The largest, most popular ETF is the SPDR Gold Trust (GLD). They purchase 400-ounce gold bars from London Good Delivery, and they issue shares at one-tenth of the price of an ounce of gold, so shares are affordable.

Companies who sell physical gold to the public are quick to note the downside to ETFs: in the event of a complete market meltdown, holders of ETFs will be left with no physical gold and shares in funds that are probably worth very little.

Another way to invest in gold is to purchase stock in gold-mining companies. *MiningNerds.com* and *24hgold.com* are two excellent sites with loads of information about mining companies. Keep in mind, however, that the performance of mining companies does not track with the spot price of gold.

What Is the "Good Delivery" Standard?

The London Bullion Market Association is one of the world's top organizations that regulate the gold industry. Members of the LBMA have a compiled list of accredited melters and assayers whose gold and silver bars they accept without question, without the need for further testing, or assaying. Such bars earn the distinction of "London Good Delivery" status. Good Delivery bars are the standard for gold that is bought and sold on the wholesale market between central banks, gold and silver producers, refiners, fabricators, and other large-scale traders throughout the world. Most ETFs own Good Delivery bars. The LBMA was formally incorporated in 1987 in close consultation with the Bank of England. The Good Delivery designation is a way for wholesalers to trust the quality of the product they are trading.

The London Good Delivery gold bar must have a minimum fineness of 995.0 and a gold content of between 350 and 430 fine ounces with the bar weight expressed in multiples of 0.025 of an ounce (the smallest weight used in the market). Bars are generally close to 400 ounces or 12.5 kilograms.

In order to achieve this distinction, refiners must meet a list of stringent requirements, including an established record of at least three years of producing the refined metal for which they are seeking certification, producing a minimum of the metal per year (10 tons of gold and 30 tons of silver), having a certifiable net worth of the equivalent of 10 million pounds, and letters of endorsement from a central bank.

> The LBMA Good Delivery List is now widely recognized as representing the de facto standard for the quality of gold and silver bars, in large part thanks to their stringent requirements.

What Is the Spot Price?

The most recognized gold price comes from the COMEX (Commodity Exchange) located in New York. The COMEX is the leading commodity exchange in the United States for metals. It is a division of the NYMEX (New York Mercantile Exchange). The process of determining spot gold prices on the COMEX is specified in the NYMEX "Rule Book."

The real-time, second by second, spot price of gold is the price of the futures contract of the "most active month" as it is trading on the exchange. The most active nearby month is called the "spot month." Even though there are contracts for every month of the year, some contracts are only lightly traded. In order to get an accurate spot gold and silver price the exchange uses the most active nearby month.

What's the Difference Between Coins, Bars, and Bullion?

"Bullion" is a comprehensive term that refers to gold in its most basic form, which is valued at its carat weight, without any additional value. Bullion can be in the form of coins or bars, but the coins do not have additional intrinsic value based on qualities such as rarity or condition. Coins that have additional value are said to be "numismatic," which means they are collectible based on scarcity or condition. In the unlikely event that gold is confiscated by the federal government, numismatic coins are exempt from confiscation. (We will look into this further in subsequent chapters, but if you stop reading here and decide to go buy a few rare gold coins, remember that the markup for collectible coins is often far greater than what the market will actually support. Be especially wary of "Last Chance!" online sales or high-pressure sales techniques.)

Buying Gold

There are two primary ways to buy physical gold: online, or at a storefront.

Either way, gold and other metals will show two prices: "bid" or "ask."

The bid price is what the dealer will pay you for a certain coin; the ask price is what the dealer is charging you. In some cases there can be a wide disparity between the bid price and the ask price, especially for numismatic, or collectible, coins.

This is from the website of *Goldline.com*:

> "Goldline's 'bid' is the price it pays to clients for a product. Goldline's 'ask' is the price it charges clients for a product. Goldline has a price differential or 'spread' between its bid (buy-back) and ask (selling) prices for precious metals, rare coins and rare currency. Prices may fluctuate throughout the day depending on the product. Pricing is based on many factors including Goldline's assessment

of world market conditions, overhead and other considerations. The price of Goldline's semi-numismatic and numismatic coins and currency include the bid/ask spread that ranges between 30% and 35%. A typical spread on bullion coins is approximately 4% to 6%. Goldline's minimum buy/sell/liquidation/delivery commission is currently $15 per trade. With the exception of the most common 1 oz. bullion coins, Goldline charges clients its numismatic spread on coins and currency. Examples of coins which have a spread between 30% and 35% include the Swiss 20 Franc, the First Strike certified coins, the Morgan and Peace silver dollars in all grades, all proof coins, and the Walking Liberty, Franklin and Kennedy silver half-dollars in all grades."

So, you can buy a coin from Goldline and turn around to sell it back to them the next day, and you pay $30 in transaction fees plus a potential loss of 35 percent. So, if you buy a numismatic coin for $1,000 on Monday, on Tuesday Goldline will buy it back for $650, minus $30 for transaction fees, or $620.

Purchasing Gold Online

If you choose to purchase gold online, you'll find a wide variety of prices, services offered, and options.

www.GoldPrice.org offers real-time price comparisons on a wide variety of gold coins and bars, so you can compare prices easily. You can also compare the brokerage fees and shipping fees.

Some companies, such as *GoldMoney.com*, store the gold in vaults for customers; you cannot buy gold from them directly and have it shipped to you.

Others, such as *Goldline.com*, will either ship your gold to you or store it for a fee.

Paying for gold storage can quickly eat into the value of your investment. While the price of gold may rise, it may also fall; it's better to view owing gold as a secure way to *store* wealth, but not primarily as a way to *create* wealth. Remember the adage about an ounce of gold being worth the amount of a high-quality man's suit. An ounce of gold won't suddenly be able to buy two men's suits, for example. It is a store of wealth, a way to protect dollars from inflation or currency devaluation.

With this in mind, paying someone else to store your gold is a surefire way to have your principle eaten into. You won't get a bill for storing your gold: instead, your balance sheet with the company holding your gold will reflect a smaller amount of gold you own (minus the fees your pay regularly).

This is why a safer, surer bet is to have the gold in your possession.

Now, Where To Put It?

So, you've bought gold. Maybe you have a few coins or bars. Now, where to put it?

If you ask three different people, you'll get three different answers, but many have a generalized suspicion of safety deposit boxes. If you ever have a judgment against you or you owe the government, then it is possible that the contents of the box could be seized. There is also historical precedent for safety deposit boxes being seized in the event of a bank failure.

What about gold vaults?

While many are built like Fort Knox, the reality is that, in times of national emergency, gold theoretically could be confiscated. The possibility is remote, but, if you're buying gold as a hedge against the unthinkable, then you'll probably want to be as conservative as possible.

Some advocate storing the gold in offshore vaults. There are reputable, well-known vaults in Vienna and Hong Kong, for example. Many online sellers store the gold, for a fee, in offshore vaults. *GoldMoney.com*, for example, has vaults in London, Zurich, and Hong Kong.

Storage fees for safekeeping in vaults typically run from .015% of holdings a month or .018% of holdings for a year. Some have a $5/month minimum. You pay the fee for every vault, so if you store gold in three different vaults, even if the vaults are owned by the same company, then you pay three different fees. The amount owed is usually not billed but is subtracted from the value of the account, which means that the actual gold in your name dwindles over time.

When you buy gold and have it stored for you, you can buy either **allocated** or **unallocated** gold. **Allocated** means that you buy an actual, physical portion of gold, usually a bar. You receive the serial number, and the gold is stored under your name. It is yours. You own it, and the bank cannot sell it, liquidate it, or loan it out to someone else. Unallocated means that the seller/storer/bank owns gold as an asset, so if the bank runs into financial difficulties, that asset would be liquidated and you would get in line as a creditor. For this reason, allocated gold is pricier; you pay a little more than the "spot price," and in return you have the security of actual gold possession.

What Is Bailment?

What if the privately-owned vault goes out of business? Is your gold protected?

When you pay to have *allocated* gold stored for you in a secure vault, that gold is protected by *bailment*, which is the legal action of a client entrusting their bullion to another party for safekeeping. Bailment describes a legal relationship in common law where physical possession of personal property such as bullion is transferred from one person or entity (the "bailor" or client) to another person or entity (the "bailee" or company) who subsequently holds possession of the bullion. Importantly, precious metals remain the property of the investor. This eliminates counter party and intermediation risk posed by business failure and company insolvency.

Owning bullion in this way gives you the soundest protection from company insolvency.

When companies fail, liquidators are appointed and take control of the company's assets, sell them, and arrange a fair distribution of the assets to creditors of various classes. Liquidators generally claim ownership of every asset on a failed company's balance sheet, including bullion. However, they cannot lawfully treat bailments as the property of the company available for creditors' benefit.

Through bailment, an individual gives up possession of their bullion but remains the outright legal owner of their bullion, with the investment provider acting simply as a custodian.

Arguments for Self-Storage

In the event of a global financial collapse, you probably don't want your wealth sitting in a vault in Geneva. A case can be made for keeping some gold close at hand.

Some argue that a fireproof safe is a good bet. Building it into a hidden wall is not a bad idea, or storing it in the attic. There's always the possibility that a robber holds a gun to your head and demands that you unlock the safe, so hide the safe.

If you're determined to hide the gold from everyone, to hide all evidence, to make sure that no one but you knows where it is, then seal it in PVC pipe and bury it in the back yard (away from power, water, or sewer lines that might provide an unexpected bonanza for some lucky utility worker). Just remember where you bury it, and provide instructions somewhere for your family in the event of an untimely demise (yours).

Jewelry Basics

Moving on, let's look at jewelry. You may have an old gold chain or two lying around, an old ring, maybe a few mismatched earrings. How can you convert this to as much cash as possible?

How Is Gold Jewelry Valued?

In jewelry, the purity of gold is expressed in 24ths, or karats: 24-karat gold is pure, 12-karat is 50-percent gold, and so on. Most gold jewelry is 14 carat; some other metal has been added, because 24-carat gold is extremely soft and is easily marred or dented.

When you take gold jewelry in to be evaluated, most jewelers will want to perform a simple chemical test to verify the actual gold content. The test usually involves either running the piece across a slightly abraded surface then testing the residue, or making a very fine scratch on the piece (on the back or underside, so it's not visible), then applying a chemical that reacts depending on the percentage of gold in the piece.

The gold is then weighed. A determination of value is made by three factors: weight, actual gold content, and the current price of gold.

It is important to note that, when you sell jewelry in this manner, what you are getting is the melt value only; the value of any craftsmanship is lost.

Pennyweights (dwt), Grams, or Troy Ounces… What's the Difference?

The *Troy ounce* is the traditional unit of weight used for precious metals. The term derives from the French town of Troyes, where this unit was first used in the Middle Ages. One troy ounce is equal to 1.0971428 ounces by weight. In the bullion market, all references to ounces mean troy ounces.

Other common units of measure:

1 **gram** = 0.03 of a troy ounce

Pennyweight (dwt) = 1/20 of a troy ounce, or 1.5 grams

To get a sense of comparison, one U.S. quarter weighs 3.5 pennyweight.

Selling Gold

The key to maximizing profits when you sell gold is to eliminate as many middlemen as possible in the transaction.

If you sell gold to a dealer in a storefront, for example, he will turn around and sell that gold to a wholesale smelter or fabricator. If you sell your gold at a gold party, then you've just added one or maybe two people taking a cut of proceeds. Throw in a glass or two of wine and you may find yourself royally ripped off.

The key, then, is to find a smelter or refiner and sell your gold to them directly. They will melt down your gold, separating it into its component materials, then they will either pay you (usually 2% less than the spot price), or, they will charge a small fee and return the materials to you in their purified forms. Google the closest major city and the term "gold refiner."

In order to sell your gold to a refiner, you'll need a tax ID number (for tax purposes). The next best alternative is to find a reputable dealer who has been around, has a nice storefront, and won't be gone at daylight. Remember, the goal is to eliminate as many people as possible between you and the refiner.

Above all, avoid the little, tawdry storefronts with the enormous "We Buy Gold!" banners. The crummier the building, the less you'll get for your gold.

Instead, look for a reputable gold and silver exchange that has been in business for many years, preferably decades.

When you take your gold in, if it's scrap gold, such as loose earrings or old jewelry, expect the dealer to ask to test your gold for purity. A simple chemical test can tell if the gold is 10, 14, 18, or 24-carat (pure) gold, or if it's gold plated, or not gold at all.

Next, the gold will be weighed on an extremely sensitive scale.

An offer will be made on the spot that factors in the weight and percentage of gold in the items you are selling.

Expect discrepancies in what dealers are willing to pay—sometimes wide discrepancies.

One morning I took a small ring and bracelet in to three different shops near Dallas, Texas, all within a five-mile radius. The jewelry weighed 8.9 dwt (pennyweight). Within a few hours I was offered $200, $275, and $288—for the exact same pieces. One dealer (the one who offered the least) suggested that the gold was mixed with copper, even though two previous dealers had performed a chemical test and verified that both were 14-carat gold.

The point is that those who buy gold are *often* unscrupulous.

Another trend to avoid is mailing your gold off, where it is presumably tested and weighed and a check is sent to you "promptly." (If this is truly your last resort, you're bedridden and have no friends or family to help, you live in the Arctic, and you need to raise funds quickly, look into *www.Cash4Gold.com*.) Some refiners also accept gold by mail. But use this as a last resort. You'll get more for your money through a reputable dealer, without the laundry list of *things that can go wrong* when you put your gold in the mail. Plus, you'll have the option of deciding *not* to sell, and you'll still be in physical possession of your gold.

Gold IRAs

Since the passage of the Tax Payer Relief Act of 1997, gold and other precious metals can now be included in retirement portfolio holdings such as IRAs.

According to *SmartMoney.com*, the Internal Revenue Code allows IRAs to own certain gold, silver and platinum coins, as well as gold, silver, platinum and palladium bullion that meet applicable fineness standards. For example, an IRA can own American Gold Eagle coins, Canadian Gold Maple Leaf coins, American Silver Eagle coins, American Platinum Eagle coins and gold and silver bars (bullion) that are 99.9% pure or better. Some well-known gold coins, including the South African Krugerrand, are off limits, as are bullion bars that are not sufficiently pure.

The coins or bullion must be held by the IRA trustee rather than the IRA owner. In other words, you can't have your IRA buy coins or bullion and stash them in your safe deposit box or bury them in your backyard. These tax rules apply equally to traditional IRAs, Roth IRAs, simplified employee pension (SEP) accounts and Simple IRAs.

The big issue with IRA ownership of precious metal assets is finding a trustee that is willing to set up a self-directed IRA, handle the transfer of funds to the precious metals dealer and facilitate the physical transfer and storage of the coins or bullion. Only a handful of brokerage firms allow gold IRAs.

The trustee will typically charge a one-time IRA set-up fee, an annual management fee for producing account statements and handling other paperwork, and an annual fee for storing and insuring the coins or bullion. Additional fees may be charged for various transactions, including account contributions and distributions and purchases and sales of coin or bullion. The IRA owner is usually on his own when it comes to finding a precious metals dealer to sell coins or bullion to the IRA or to buy coins or bullion from the account. Examples of such dealers include USAGOLD-Centennial Precious Metals and Goldline International.

Indirect Precious Metal Investments via ETFs, ETNs, and Mining Stocks

One option for those who are uncomfortable with having their IRAs own coins or bullion is buying shares of an exchange traded fund

(ETF) that tracks the value of particular precious metals. Two of the most-popular precious metals ETFs are the **SPDR Gold Trust** and the **iShares Silver Trust**; both have been approved by the IRS. (If you have doubts about your IRA being allowed to own an ETF, read the tax section of the fund's prospectus, which should be available online.) A potentially more risky option is an exchange traded note (ETN), an unsecured type of bank note based on a particular index.

Another indirect way of investing in precious metals is to have your IRA buy stock in a mining company. For example, your IRA could buy shares in **Barrick Gold Corporation**, the world's largest pure gold mining company. There are no tax concerns with this option.

Incorporating holdings in gold into your IRA takes advantage of other IRA benefits, including:

- Defer taxes on your earnings so that you can potentially accumulate more for retirement.

- Invest annually up to $5,000, or $6,000 if you're age 50 or older.
- Supplement your 401(k) retirement plan savings.

The *Kitco Gold Index*: U.S. Dollar Strength and the Price of Gold

The price of gold fluctuates, but so does the value of the U.S. dollar. The Kitco Gold Index is a tool that can help investors determine the real value of gold on the global market, taking into consideration fluctuations in the value of the dollar against other currencies.

When the U.S. dollar gets stronger, it takes fewer dollars to buy any commodity that is priced in $USD. When the U.S. dollar gets weaker it takes more dollars to purchase the same commodity, according to analysts at *Kitco.com*.

> "The price of all U.S. dollar denominated commodities, like gold, will change to reflect the fact that it will take fewer or more dollars to buy that commodity. So it's quite possible,

in fact it's almost always the case that a portion of the change in the price of gold is really just a reflection of a change in the value of the U.S. dollar....

"If gold is higher in U.S. dollars while at the same time cheaper in every other currency, then we can conclude that the U.S. dollar has weakened, and that gold has actually lost value in all other currencies. But the price, because it is being quoted in $USD will be higher and give the illusion of gold becoming more valuable. In such a case the devaluation of gold, due to increased supply on the market, is camouflaged by a weakened U.S. dollar."

One very useful feature on *Kitco.com* breaks the change of the price of gold into two components. One part shows you how much of that change can be attributed to U.S. dollar strength (or lack of it). The other portion is indicative of how much the price changed as a result of normal trading. Interestingly, whatever changes happen to the price of gold as a result of U.S. dollar strength/weakness also occurs to every other U.S. dollar-denominated commodity by the exact same proportion. (To see this index, Google *Kitco gold index*.)

Wedding Season in India?

November and December are traditional wedding months in India, and the festival of Diwali is usually held toward the end of October, so this is the time when demand for gold usually spikes in India. (Gold is a common wedding gift for brides in India, and a family's wealth is often displayed by the gold worn by both men and women during these festivities.) This traditionally means that demand (and the price) of gold rises during this period.

However, most gold in India is imported, which means that currency prices can affect the price of gold in India. When the rupee is devalued, or when the dollar is strong, this can make gold prohibitively expensive. In the fall of 2011, when the dollar was very strong against the rupee, the demand for gold plummeted. Instead of strong new purchasing, families sold old gold pieces or scrap gold, to take advantage of high market value.

When gold is at or near a high, and when currency values play a significant role, the old assumptions about gold can be challenged in international markets.

What About China?

China is increasingly a player in the global demand for gold. Although China is the world's largest producer of gold, it remains tightly controlled by the People's Bank of China. Much of the investment in gold in China is speculative; buyers tend to sell when the price rises, which keeps the gold in circulation. If the PRC ever decided to buy and hold gold, the price would certainly skyrocket.

Forbes' contributor Robert Lenzner is bullish on China's effect on gold. "Get ready for the Pan Asian Gold Exchange, scheduled to open in June 2012, in Kunming City, Yunman

Province– the gateway to all of Southeast Asia. This is serious, as the Pan Asian Gold Exchange is a part of China's five-year plan–which means it is part of China's strategy for dominance in global financial markets and the global economy.

"Pan Asian will allow the Chinese to speculate in gold futures contracts or buy physical gold through an account with a bank or broker. All 320 million customers of the giant Agricultural Bank of China will simply be able to use their Renminbi, the Chinese currency, from their bank accounts to trade gold." This means that the Chinese impact on the gold market could factor in significantly, soon.

Pitfalls To Avoid When Buying or Selling Gold

- Paying unnecessary or hidden fees.

- Failing to understand the value of your gold (weight, gold content) before you try to sell it.

- Failing to comparison shop.

- Buying on a whim.

- Buying with money that you will need in the short term.

- Hidden costs that decimate returns.

- Buying expensive, rare coins instead of bullion.

What About Silver?

Like gold, silver is quite useful as a metal and has many uses beyond coins and jewelry; it is commonly used in dentistry, manufacturing, and as a component of photo processing.

Silver typically sells in the $10-50 range. $10 is a bargain; $50 is very high. For more than two decades silver sold for less than $10 an ounce, but since about 2004 silver has begun a (relatively) steady climb. Silver currently sells in the $30-35 range; www.GoldPrice.org is a good site to get instant quotes for silver as well as gold.

There are generally two types of silver: sterling silver and fine silver. Sterling silver is .925 pure; an alloy is added, usually copper, to provide added strength. Sterling silver is generally used for tableware, serving pieces, and some jewelry. Fine silver is .995 to .999 pure. Silver coins, bars and ingots are usually fine silver.

Silver tends to rise and fall in a somewhat parallel trend with gold, but an added benefit is that silver is much less expensive. As with gold, be sure to comparison shop and compare premiums and added costs.

Morgan Dollars

The most well-known collectible silver coin is the Morgan dollar, which has a fascinating history that involved the period in which the U.S. Government was attempting to establish a gold standard, yet was confounded by obligations to miners in the West who were sitting on vast silver mines, including the fabled Comstock Lode.

More than half a *billion* Morgan dollars were minted between 1878 and 1904, and although nearly three-fourths of these were melted back down before being issued, the majority of the Morgans in the marketplace today didn't even leave the Mint until 1960. The bottom line is that Morgan dollars in uncirculated grades are very, very common, so keep this in mind when contemplating the purchase of Morgans. (Less-than-honest dealers might lead you to believe that just because the Morgan dollar is old, the fact that it's in mint condition makes it very valuable. The truth is that MS-63 specimens for about half the mint/date combinations sell for $35 to $70 each. Some well-known but unscrupulous dealers ask $350 to $700 for the same coins.)

A Short History of How the Hunt Brothers Cornered the Silver Market

In the 1970s, the Hunt brothers, Nelson "Bunker" Hunt and William "Herbert" Hunt, oil barons from Houston, Texas, created havoc in the silver market. Swayed by conspiracy theories, the Hunt brothers speculated, hoarded, conspired to corner the market, miscalculated, and ended up in bankruptcy (and jail).

Before it was all over with, the Hunts had hoarded almost 10 percent of the world's availably supply of silver and had driven the price from $1.50 in 1970 to $50 in 1980. When the bubble burst and the price adjusted to $21, the Hunts had margin calls they couldn't meet. The Hunts had assets of $1.5 billion but liabilities of $2.5 billion—making them the greatest individual debtors in the history of finance. In 1988, Nelson Bunker Hunt filed personal bankruptcy and was convicted of illegally attempting to corner the market in silver.

Silver Scams To Watch Out For

Almost any "commemorative" coin is virtually guaranteed to be ridiculously overpriced. For example, one company "mints" silver coins with the symbols of popular college sports teams. On a day when one ounce of silver was $32, the one-ounce "commemorative" coins were selling for $99. Buy them as a novelty if you must, but not as an investment.

Chapter 3: Numismatics – What You Need To Know About How Coins Are Valued

The term "numismatics" refers to coins whose value is based on factors such as condition, grade, scarcity, and demand, rather than their metal content. In other words, numismatics refers to coin collecting, as opposed to collecting gold and silver purely as instruments of wealth. The business of coin collecting and investing in rare or valuable coins is filled with danger for the novice investor.

Before buying numismatic coins, do some research. Buy the blue book and the red book.

The *what*?

The **Blue Book** is the widely accepted wholesale price guide for U.S. coins. The formal title is *Handbook of United States Coins*, published by Whitman Books. The Blue Book price is generally the amount you can expect a coin dealer to pay you for your coins. The **Red Book**, also published by Whitman, is the retail price the dealer plans to sell your coins for. Both books provide thousands of photos and can serve as a guide to tell you what a coin is really worth.

The Sheldon Scale (below) is the very specific set of guidelines that coin graders use to determine the value of a coin.

The Sheldon Scale for Grading U.S. Coins

Poor-1 or P-1 (Poor) -- The type is barely discernible due to the coin being badly damaged or worn smooth.

Fair-2 or FR-2 (Fair) -- Type and date are barely discernible, but otherwise the coin is damaged or extremely worn.

AG-3 (About Good) -- Type and date are discernible, although some spots may be worn out. Some lettering should be apparent, if not necessarily readable.

G-4 (Good) -- Major devices and features are evident as outlines, although the coin is heavily worn.

G-6 (Good-plus) -- Coin has a full rim plus major devices and features are clearly outlined. Heavy wear.

VG-8 (Very Good) -- Full rim with clearly discernible devices and features. Most legends are readable clearly, but the whole coin is still significantly worn.

F-12 (Fine) -- Distinct rim, all legends readable, clear devices showing some detail, but the whole coin is moderately (but evenly) worn.

VF-20 (Very Fine) -- Clearly readable but lightly worn legends, devices show good detail, rims are clean, but the whole coin shows moderate wear on the high points and a little wear below.

VF-30 (Good Very Fine) -- Legends are clear, devices show all detail with little wear; high points are lightly worn.

EF-40 (Extremely Fine) -- Legends are sharp, devices are clear with slight but obvious wear on the high points.

XF-45 (Choice Extremely Fine) -- Legends and devices are clear and sharp, with slight wear on the high points, and great eye appeal.

AU-50 (About Uncirculated) -- Sharp legends and devices show only a trace of wear on the highest points. There must be some remaining mint luster.

AU-55 (Good About Uncirculated) -- Sharp legends and devices show only a hint of wear on the high points. Remaining mint luster must be at least half; great eye appeal.

AU-58 (Choice About Uncirculated) -- Virtually uncirculated, except for minor wear marks on high points. Nearly all mint luster must be present, and must have outstanding eye appeal.

MS-60 (Mint State Basal) -- Coins in this grade are ugly, dinged-up, bag-marked, ill-toned specimens, but they are in mint condition and free of any wear.

MS-70 – Perfect condition, uncirculated.

The grades from MS-60 to MS-70, as well as the Proof designations, are all based primarily on eye appeal, quality of luster and/or toning, and the presence or absence of contact marks, hairlines, and so forth. All coins MS-60 and higher are Mint State coins. ("Proof" is not a grade, but a type of coin.)

The Business of Grading Coins

Grading coins is big business. There are many companies that grade coins, and some use more exacting standards than others. When a company grades a coin they encapsulate it in a protective plastic cover, called a *slab*, and it is stamped with the grade and the company that graded it.

Coin grading and encapsulation services are generally regarded as belonging to one of three tiers:

- Top Tier -- PCGS and NGC

- Second Tier -- ANACS and ICG

- Third Tier -- All others, including ACG, INB, NTC, PCI, SEGS, and SGS

Both PCGS and NGC are very highly regarded for their conservative and consistent grading. Be cautious if you see sellers claiming PCGS prices for coins in any other grading company's slab.

The "Graded Coin Value" Fraud

According to Susan Headley at *About.com*, buying coins from online auction sites such as eBay can be a good way to find a bargain, but it can also be a good way to get ripped off. One of the most rampant coin-related frauds online is the "graded coin value" fraud.

The graded coin value fraud works like this: The unscrupulous seller will post an auction for a coin that has been graded by a "third tier" grading service, and then claim the value of the coin according to PCGS graded values. This is frequently done in lots; you'll see a photo of a small collection that the seller claims he inherited or bought at an estate sale. The photo will usually have several encapsulated coins in it. The seller will then link to, or quote, PCGS values for these coins as if they had been graded and encapsulated by PCGS, when in fact, the coins are greatly over-graded and in third tier slabs.

For example, a seller will list an encapsulated 1968-D business strike Washington Quarter, graded MS-68. He will encourage potential bidders to visit the PCGS coin values page to verify his claim that the coin is worth $8,000 in MS-68. The buyer checks PCGS; sure enough, the 1968-D MS-68 quarter is listed for $8,000. His asking price of $400 is seemingly a bargain. After all, the coin is graded and slabbed.

But there's a problem. The problem is that the coin was graded by SGS. SGS (Star Grading Service) is a "third tier" service that, according to its website, "specializes in grades 60 through 70." Apparently, these are the only grades they issue. So, a coin graded by PCGS as AU-50 would grade somewhere between MS-60 and MS-70 at Star.

Each grading service has its own standards, and just because SGS grades a coin MS-68 does not make it worth the same amount of money as a coin graded by PCGS as MS-68. The reason for this is that PCGS has very conservative grading standards. If PCGS value is claimed, but the coin is not in a PCGS slab, be skeptical. If it's not in a PCGS holder, PCGS values do not apply.

Numismatic Collecting and the Fear Factor

In 1933, President Franklin D. Roosevelt issued Executive Order 6102 that confiscated (and paid for) all privately owned gold, excepting coins with numismatic value. Why was this deemed necessary, and could it happen again?

Some say yes, that the federal government, in a time of dire crisis, could again confiscate gold.

Most experts, however, argue that the reason gold was confiscated in the 1930s was because the U.S. Government was on a gold standard at the time. Gold was the real collective wealth of the United States, and U.S. Treasury gold reserves were dwindling to an alarming rate. It was theoretically possible that runs on banks and foreign countries that owned U.S. dollars and bonds could collectively trade in their cash for gold and bankrupt the United States. (This, incidentally, is one excellent reason why returning to the gold standard is a bad idea.)

By making the transition to a fiat currency, the United States has effectively returned gold and gold ownership to the private sector.

The argument that is made by some, however, for collecting coins with numismatic value—that is, coins that are valued for qualities beyond their actual metal content—is that Executive Order 6102 specifically exempted collectible coins from the gold confiscation. It was physically too difficult to value such collectibles, since their value was far above melt value, so they became impractical sources for gold confiscation.

This is one argument you'll hear again and again for purchasing numismatic coins: The government can't take them!

The reality, however, is that the market for numismatic coins can be arbitrary. While some coins are undeniably valuable, and there are entire reference books available for helping to determine the value of numismatic coins, they are far less liquid than bullion. Before a high-value, collectible coin can be sold, you first must find a buyer. If you are holding coins as a hedge against global economic collapse, then odds are good that, in the midst of societal upheaval, it might be challenging to find a buyer for an exquisite, rare coin. The value is in the eye of the beholder, and the purchaser. In short, the value is somewhat subjective. Once the threat of government confiscation of bullion is removed, owning coins of numismatic value becomes more of a hobby.

A final word of caution about numismatic coins: when shopping for numismatic coins, dealers will give you two prices: the offer or call price (what you would pay for the coin) and the sell or put price (what they would pay you for the coin).

For example, the offer price for a specific numismatic coin on XYZ.com might be $500. This is what you pay if you want to buy the coin (not including shipping, handling, insurance, and maybe storage).

The sell price on that exact same coin could easily be $300. So if you buy the coin for $500 on Monday, have buyer's remorse on Tuesday and want to sell it back, you've already lost at least $200.

Contrast this with buying and selling bullion, which tracks the spot price of gold very closely. You may buy a 1-oz. coin on Monday and sell it on Tuesday, and there will be no subjective factors involved in the transaction. The market determines the value, not the opinion or cash position of the buyer.

On a Practical Note...

If you have a numismatic coin, the one thing you should never, ever do is clean it. This is the coin-collecting equivalent of refinishing antique furniture, or repainting a collectible car. It strips away a considerable amount of value. If the coin looks worn or tarnished or has a patina, leave it alone. It's worth more that way.

Chapter 4: The Tarnished Side of the Business

From unscrupulous sellers to counterfeiters, the business of precious metals has always attracted some less-than-wholesome elements. Counterfeits from China are beginning to be seen in relatively large quantities, and they range from common coins in small denominations to replicas of numismatic coins all the way to fake gold and silver bars.

Another tarnished side of the business is the problem of unscrupulous dealers. They will sell coins for far more than they are worth, and they will buy coins for far less. They rely on the perception of expertise, and in many cases they prey on the vulnerable.

One dealer tells of his frustration at coin shows of seeing unscrupulous dealers. "A little old lady will come in with a jar full of old coins. The dealer will barely glance up, then will mutter something like, 'I'll give you 10 percent above face value—that's all it's worth.' In reality the dealer is hoping for a score, to find one or more coins of great value in the lady's collection. A conscientious dealer would take five minutes and look at her coins carefully, and give her a fair price."

Other forms of deception are common. What you can get for scrap gold, for example, can vary widely depending on the integrity of the buyer.

Conspiracy Theories Abound

The Great Gold Conspiracy

The basic idea of the Great Gold Conspiracy is that banks and investment firms have colluded to keep the price of gold artificially low. An investor who "discovers" this hidden agenda thus has a chance to beat the proverbial system and make money in spite of powerful financial interests.

"The basic notion of the gold conspiracy theory is that the central banks and major firms have colluded to artificially suppress the price of gold, much to their mutual benefit. Whether true or not, this theory feeds the fantasy of the small speculator uncovering a cartel of bandits and using this knowledge to make his fortune. It is David and Goliath all over again," says economist Eric Noel.

Proponents of owning (and physically possessing) gold, or gold bugs, refer to those who would act to keep prices artificially low as "the Cartel." It's a vague, sinister-sounding group.

But Noel sees no difference in gold and other commodities. "In my humble view, gold trades no differently than any other commodity such as sugar, coffee, oil or even lean hogs. All of these markets adhere to basic price structure limits and Fibonacci projections in the same exact way. Thus, if gold is being manipulated, would it not be expected to behave differently than the other commodities?"

Suspicions About the Fed

A common misconception is that the Federal Reserve, or "the Fed," is a privately owned banking system owned by very powerful, supersecret elite. The complexity of the U.S. (and, indeed, global) banking system lends itself to suspicion that it's an elaborate ruse.

In reality, the Federal Reserve is a banking structure composed of the presidentially appointed Board of Governors (or Federal Reserve Board), the Federal Open Market Committee (FOMC), 12 regional Federal Reserve Banks located in major cities throughout the nation, numerous privately owned U.S. member banks and various advisory councils.

According to the Board of Governors, the Federal Reserve is independent within government in that its decisions do not have to be ratified by the President or anyone else in the executive or legislative branch of government. However, its authority is derived from the U.S. Congress and is subject to congressional oversight. (www.federalreserve.gov).

The Federal Reserve is responsible for carrying out many of the federal laws that protect consumers in their dealings with banks and financial institutions. The Board of Governors, located in Washington, D.C., works with the 12 Federal Reserve banks around the country to make certain that the commercial banks which the Federal Reserve supervises abide by these laws. As a federal regulatory agency, the Federal Reserve System investigates consumer complaints received against State-chartered banks that are members of the System. Complaints or problems with banks and financial institutions that are not supervised by the Federal Reserve System are referred to the appropriate federal agency.

Although the Federal Reserve takes actions to set monetary policy on a macroeconomic scale, it also serves a role as a form of a consumer protection service, ensuring that its banks treat customers fairly and consistently. The Federal Reserve can help individual consumers by answering questions about banking practices, and investigating complaints and problems with specific banks under its jurisdiction.

But what does the Federal Reserve actually *do*?

The main job of the Federal Reserve is to set interest rates via the discount rate, or the federal funds rate, or the rates that banks lend to each other. In this way the Fed manages the money supply, by either loosening or constricting the available amount of credit within the U.S. banking system.

According to USMint.gov, the money supply is further regulated through the supply of coin and cash. The U.S. Mint ships the coins that it produces to the Federal Reserve banks for distribution into the economy through the banking system. The money produced by the Treasury Department (both coinage and currency) is placed into and removed out of circulation through the Federal Reserve banks and their branches. When individuals or businesses want currency or coins to spend, they write a check, exchanging one form of money (checkbook money) for another (cash). Banks satisfy this demand with "purchases" of cash from Federal Reserve banks. This is done with special checkbook money called a reserve balance. As this newly obtained cash is spent, it flows back into the banking system as business and individual deposits. When banks accumulate more cash than they need for day-to-day transactions, they deposit it into the bank's checking account at the local Federal Reserve bank. Sometimes the Federal Reserve banks need additional money to replace currency notes that are unfit for circulation or to meet expanding demand. They then place orders with the U.S. Mint and the Bureau of Engraving and Printing.

According to *Investopedia.com*, "the Department of the Treasury and the Federal Reserve work together in an effort to maintain a stable economy. The Federal Reserve serves as the government's banker, processing transactions, such as accepting electronic payments for Social Security taxes, issuing payroll checks to government employees and clearing checks for tax payments and other government receivables."

The Federal Reserve and the Department of the Treasury also work together to borrow money when the government needs to raise cash. The Federal Reserve issues U.S. Treasury securities and conducts Treasury securities auctions, selling these securities on behalf of the

Department of the Treasury. Examples of Treasury securities include Treasury bonds, bills, and notes.

How Is the Dollar Valued?

The dollar is valued in three ways. The first is against its value to other countries' currencies, through the exchange rate. This fluctuates daily, and is related to the CPI, or Consumer Price Index, which is the value of a conceptualized basket of goods and services. The CPI helps determine the rate of inflation. Second, the dollar's value is measured by Treasury notes, which can be converted easily into dollars, and are auctioned daily. Third, the dollar's value is measured by foreign currency reserves. This is the amount of dollars held by foreign governments.

The Market of Fear

There is a very real component of fear in the world of buying and selling gold. There are many who have a complete distrust of the government and assume that an enormous conspiracy exists, the goal of which is to gain complete world domination.

You don't have to go far to find those who hold such views.

Glenn Beck is one popular purveyor of fear. His "Three G's formula" (God, Gold, Guns) is a succinct summary of the mindset of a person who is, above all, mistrustful of government and often society in general.

In exploring the world of gold and gold dealers, one dealer in particular stood out to me as an example of this mindset. While writing this book, I visited many shops and storefronts, to get quotes on scrap gold, and just to talk with dealers in general about the market.

This particular dealer had a locked door, as most do, but as he unlocked the front door to let me in he revealed a shoulder holster and a gun.

I showed him the scrap gold I had, he tested it and weighed it, and we started talking.

"You know the government doesn't want you to own gold, don't you?" he asked.

"Why is that?"

"Because then they can't control you. They can't control the value of what you possess. You know they've confiscated gold before, right?"

I did know that.

"Well, who's to say they won't do it again?"

His eyes narrowed.

"You need to do more research, young lady," he said. "Do you know about the Bilderberg Group? The Trilateral Commission? The Illuminati? Have you read *The Creature from Jekyll Island*?"

I had not. But after our discussion I did. And this is what I found.

The Creature from Jekyll Island is an enormous tome by G. Edward Griffin that reads like a spy novel, and it recounts the origins of the Federal Reserve. It's the Bible of conspiracy theory. It recounts the secrecy around the meeting of wealthy bankers, held in 1910 on Jekyll Island off the coast of Georgia, but the book makes assumptions, a *lot* of assumptions.

The Creature from Jekyll Island tends to start with facts then veers into presupposition. For example, the fact that centralized banking has allowed for tremendous growth and prosperity in the United States is generally ignored. The fact that bankers made a lot of money from this banking structure is seen not as evidence of the value of the service they provided, but as evidence that they fleeced us all.

As the gold dealer spoke, I took notes. As he rattled off the names of supposedly nefarious groups, I wrote them down. All of them, it seemed, were a type of code, shorthand for "powerful groups who rig the system and want to rule the world."

I looked into them, one by one. Sure enough, there are groups of very powerful people who meet, sometimes privately. Whether or not their goal is world domination has yet to be seen. Undercutting the message of many of these groups, especially online, are the accompanying links, articles, and advertisements, which include information on survival gardening and food storage secrets for the End Times, water purification tablets, aliens, evidence for a hollow Earth, the war on vitamins, the "invention" of AIDS, the Georgia Guidestones, the Amero (the coinage of a theoretical monetary union between the United States, Canada, and Mexico), the Rosicrucian Brotherhood, the sinister Aleister Crowley, Freemasonry, and how to survive martial law in America.

This type of hyperbole is typical:

> "Soul-less Wall Street bankers, married to soul-less government officials, are grinding this country into a pile of bones – your bones. These murderous, money-mongering, masqueraders are currently running the largest concentration camp in the world – the United States of America. In a very short time we will all come to understand, too late for most, just what they did and how they did it. But, alas,

by that time, that vast majority of the dumbed-down, mindless Americans will either be cold cadavers or will be looking at razor wire from the inside of a government concentration camp. Then comes the pile of bones – yours….

"While China is encouraging its people to buy gold and silver to protect themselves from what is coming, here we have our consortium of carnivores, already gorged and bloated from their last feeding frenzy, now, 'too big to fail,' they are lying in wait, ready to divide the spoils-of-war for the second and final time…. Buy at least six months of food for yourself and your family, convert the electronic money you don't want to lose into gold and silver while you can, and get out of their way as best you can. There is no stopping these demons." (From *goldandsilverexchange.info*)

Here is a brief rundown of the groups that are regarded with suspicion by many gold bugs:

The Bilderberg Group

The Bilderberg Group (or Bilderberg Conference, or Bilderberg Club) is an annual, unofficial, invitation-only conference of approximately 120 to 140 guests from North America and Western Europe, most of whom are people of influence in business, government, education or industry. Meetings are closed to the public and often feature future political leaders shortly before they become household names, including Texas Governor Rick Perry. The group got its name from the first meeting, held in 1954 at the Hotel de Bilderberg in the Netherlands.

The extreme secrecy of the group makes it a prime suspect in the world of conspiracy theories. The group maintains that the secrecy allows for government and industry leaders to be completely honest and candid in their interactions, without concern that their words will be misinterpreted or spun by the media.

What issues does the group address? According to the "American Friends of Bilderberg," the 2008 agenda dealt mainly with "a nuclear-free world, cyber-terrorism,

Africa, Russia, finance, protectionism, US-EU relations, Afghanistan and Pakistan, Islam, and Iran."

As for concerns that the group amounts to a cabal that rules the world? In 2005, one Bilderberger said this: "It is unavoidable and it doesn't matter. There will always be people who believe in conspiracies, but things happen in a much more incoherent fashion. When people say this is a secret government of the world I say that if we were a secret government of the world we should be bloody ashamed of ourselves."

The Trilateral Commission

The Trilateral Commission was established in 1972 by David Rockefeller after the Bilderberg Group refused to include participants from Japan. The Commission now includes representatives from North America, Europe, and the Pacific/Asia region. The purpose of the group is to promote relations between the member regions, to develop cooperation, and to facilitate interdependence in an increasingly global marketplace. "Improvement of East-West relations" is a stated concern of the group.

Zbigniew Brzezinski, a professor at Columbia University and a Rockefeller advisor who was a specialist on international affairs, left his post to help organize the group. Other founding members included Alan Greenspan and Paul Volcker, both later heads of the Federal Reserve.

The Trilateral Commission initiated its biannual meetings schedule in October 1973 in Tokyo. In May 1976, the first plenary meeting of all of the Commission's regional groups took place in Kyoto. It was through these early meetings that the group affected its most profound influence, the integration of Japan into the global political conversation. Before these exchanges, the country was much more isolated on the international stage.

Membership is divided into numbers proportionate to each of the think tank's three regional areas. The North American continent is represented by 120 members (20 Canadian, 13 Mexican and 87 U.S. citizens). The

European group has reached its limit of 170 members from almost every country on the continent; the ceilings for individual countries are 20 for Germany, 18 for France, Italy and the United Kingdom, 12 for Spain and from one to six for the rest. At first, Asia and Oceania were represented only by Japan. However, in 2000 the Japanese group of 85 members expanded itself, becoming the Pacific Asia group, composed of 117 members: 75 Japanese, 11 South Koreans, seven Australian and New Zealand citizens, and 15 members from the ASEAN nations (Indonesia, Malaysia, Philippines, Singapore and Thailand). The Pacific Asia group also included nine members from China, Hong Kong and Taiwan. Currently, the Trilateral Commission claims "more than 100" Pacific Asian members.

Trilateral Commission bylaws exclude persons holding public office from membership; the think tank draws its participants from political, business, and academic worlds. The group is chaired by three individuals, one from each of the regions represented.

The Illuminati

The undisputed king of conspiracy theories is the fabled Illuminati, made famous by assorted books and Hollywood movies, always cloaked in a veil of extreme secrecy. The group was established in Bavaria in 1776; whether or not it truly exists today is a matter of dispute. The central idea is that a small group of powerful, wealthy individuals rules the world from behind the scenes, pulling the levers of global economics and politics to bring about a New World Order. The Freemasons are said to be a subset of the Illuminati, and Illuminati members are said to leave evidence of their presence through quite prominent symbols, such as pentagrams, triangles, and the all-seeing eye.

Popular among conspiracy theorists is the claim that the all-seeing eye, or Eye of Providence, shown atop an unfinished pyramid on the Great Seal of the United States, indicates the influence of Freemasonry in the founding of the United States. This was dramatized in the 2004 Disney film *National Treasure*. However, common Masonic use of the Eye dates to 14 years after the creation of the Great Seal. Among the members of the various design committees for the Great Seal, only Benjamin Franklin was a Mason, and his ideas for the seal were not adopted. Indeed, many Masonic organizations have explicitly denied any connection to the creation of the Seal.

Fear-Based Selling

Typical fear-based selling includes peddling the idea that this is the time to buy gold, gold prices are sure to skyrocket, and those who miss the opportunity are dim-witted. For example, an article by Franklin Sanders on *GoldPrice.com* notes: "Once silver and gold bottom... they will not revisit these prices for the rest of the bull market. That's your shot, the last train leaving the station before the Russians take Berlin, and you'd better run and catch it.

"To avoid confusion, please remember that the comments above have a very short time horizon. Always invest with the primary trend.

Gold's primary trend is up, *targeting at least $3,130.00*; silver's primary is up targeting 16:1 gold/silver ratio or $195.66; stocks' primary trend is down, targeting Dow under 2,900 and worth only one ounce of gold; US$ or US$-denominated assets, primary trend down; real estate in a bubble, primary trend way down. Whenever I write, 'Stay out of stocks' readers inevitably ask, 'Do you mean precious metals mining stocks, too?' No, I don't."

The Greater Fool Theory

There tends to be an assumption among investors that there will always be someone willing to pay more for any stock or commodity than the investor is paying. People assume they can always sell to some "greater fool" at a higher price. It's one thing to recognize that there will always be a peak, but very few consider when they buy that they may already be at that peak.

The Impact of Herd Mentality

People don't always have the best information, so they simply do what everyone else seems to be doing at the time. If the price of a commodity seems to be going up and up, there can be a desire to jump in and reap some of the wealth that is being made.

> "No warning can save people determined to grow suddenly rich."
>
> ~ *Lord Overton*

The Lure of Instant Wealth

The current market for gold is extremely volatile. With gold prices swinging wildly from day to day, there can be a temptation to buy and sell based on the very short term. While there is no doubt that day traders can (and do) do well speculating on the fluctuations on the price of gold, that type of market timing is well beyond the scope of this book. However, there are many who feel that, considering the current geo-economic instability in the world, combined with the pressure cooker of U.S. debt, long-term investing in gold is a relatively safe bet. As we've seen, gold can be an excellent way to store and preserve wealth.

What's left, then, is sorting through the maze: Finding the best ways to buy and keep gold.

Chapter 5: Our Ugly, Romantic History with Gold

What is it about gold that makes people want to own it, possess it, stockpile it, and adorn themselves with it?

The history of gold is fascinating. In this chapter we'll take a step back and learn a bit about why gold has historically been such a valuable commodity.

Man first took note of gold around 4,000 BC. By 3,000 BC, its brilliance and malleability made it useful for personal adornment, a primitive form of jewelry. The malleability of gold meant that it could be formed into thin rings and wires. It never tarnished or faded, and it looked shiny and wet even when dry.

In ancient Greece, it was thought that gold, frequently found in river and streams, was a peculiar combination of water and sunlight.

By 2,500 BC, gold was being buried with kings, and it was around that same time that gold buried with kings began to be plundered.

By 1,500 BC, hammered gold and silver coins were used for global trade.

In 1,350 BC, Babylonians began melting down gold to form pure coins. Other metals and rock were literally melted away, and the Babylonian coins became known for their purity. Trade was becoming quantifiable and standardized.

Around 1,200 BC, Egyptians discovered that they could combine melted gold with other, more durable metals, which made the resulting coins more resistant to damage.

In the 5th century BC, in the area around Georgia, east of the Black Sea, a method of extracting fine gold flakes and grains was developed using sheepskin. River water, or water flushed through mines, was poured over a sheepskin, which would trap the tiny particles. The sheepskin was then dried in the sun, then the tiny particles and flakes could be beaten from the wool, or "golden fleece."

In 561 BC, King Croesus of Lydia minted the first large-scale issue of gold coins that became the official currency of his realm.

By 320 BC, during the reign of Macedonian emperor Alexander the Great, gold became a primary cause for war, and a prominent target for plunder.

In modern times, gold has lost none of its appeal and allure.

Gold was first discovered in the United States in North Carolina in 1803. Major gold rushes occurred in 1849 in California, and in the following decade a gold rush in Australia increased the population there threefold. The last major gold rush in North America took place in the Yukon territory of Western Canada in 1897, where tens of thousands perished in their attempts to access the gold that was firmly frozen in the ground.

Tulip Mania

A bit of history that is related: In 1637, in the Netherlands, a phenomenon occurred that is known as "Tulip Mania." It is the first recorded instance of a speculative bubble.

Tulips had been introduced to the Netherlands in the 1500s from the Ottoman Empire. The Dutch were taken with the variations that could be cultivated, and possessing tulips came to be associated with great wealth and sophistication.

It has been suggested that, because Tulip Mania coincided with the height of the Bubonic Plague, there could have existed a certain type of cultural fatalism. Spending the equivalent of 10-years' wages on a single tulip bulb might not have seemed so insane when imminent death appeared likely.

Nevertheless, as prices rose steadily, many people became wealthy. Tulips went from being expensive to wildly expensive to prohibitively expensive. The crash came swiftly: in February 1637, buyers could no longer be found. People who had spent exorbitant sums on the flowers found that there was no one willing to buy them.

It was this instance of a **crowd mentality** driving up a commodity price far beyond its actual value that came to be known as the first speculative bubble. This is the definition of a speculative bubble: *When the price of something rises above its fundamental value.* Economic theorists think that people invest when they think they might "miss the boat" on the high returns that others are earning. When too many people are willing to spend more than the commodity is worth, the artificially high prices fall—usually quickly. Short-term investors are driven out, and equilibrium returns, driven by fundamental metrics rather than emotions such as fear or greed.

There have been many examples of bubbles over the past century. From the Florida real estate craze of the 1920s, to the overvalued stocks that led to the 1929 crash, to the dot-com craze of the 1980s, there exists in the minds of often unsophisticated investors the idea that they can time the market and sell before everyone else realizes that prices are no longer going up. (In the case of the 1929 stock-market crash, investors were so enthusiastic that very few—even seasoned investors—

really thought prices could fall so dramatically, so quickly, and with such dire consequences.) But it is the very nature of bubbles that they pop. Quickly.

"This is the nature of gold," says one seasoned investor. "The value of gold goes up like an escalator, but it comes down like an elevator."

What the educated investor will notice is that while commodity prices fluctuate, they often stay within a general range. Any sudden increase outside this normal range is an indication of a possible bubble.

In 2011, many commodity prices are trading far above their historical averages, according to Peter Cohan on InvestorPlace.com. "The average price of a barrel of oil between 1946 and 2011 was $18.94 a barrel. Between 2001 and 2011, oil averaged $57.02." As of December 2011, the price of oil averaged over $100, or nearly twice the decade average.

For our purposes, a similar examination of the price of gold finds similar results. The average price of gold between 1900 and 2000 was $149 an ounce. The average price of gold for the following decade, however, from 2000 to 2010, was $751 per ounce. Add just one year to that calculation, 2011, and the average price of gold from 2000 to 2011 was $939. The current price of gold, which is over $1,500, is nearly 10 times the long-term average. This means that investors are now buying not just high, but near-record high. While no one knows for sure, odds say that the price of gold is due to readjust soon.

What this means for the average investor is that this may be a great time to sell gold. (We'll examine in detail the best way to get the most for your gold in Chapter 3.)

A Rogues' Gallery

There is a veritable rogues' gallery of shady characters who populate the history of precious metals. In the past, many of those who have profited the most were those who took advantage of prospectors—the equivalent of today's small-time investors.

The #1 California Gold Rush Shady Character: Samuel Brannan

Samuel Brannan immediately recognized the profit potential in selling overpriced equipment and supplies to prospectors. Early in 1848, near Coloma, California, Brannan noticed shop customers paying for goods with small nuggets of gold they had found. Brannan reportedly purchased every shovel in San Francisco then ran through the streets, shouting "Gold! Gold has been found!"

Brannan, a Mormon, was also known to collect tithes in gold from the prospectors on behalf of the LDS Church, although whether that money ever made it to the coffers of the church is doubtful. Brannan, who was known for banding together with vigilantes to form a *de facto* police force, was eventually kicked out of the church for presumed violence.

The #1 Klondike Gold Rush Shady Character: Soapy Smith

Jefferson Randolph ("Soapy") Smith was king of the frontier con men. He started small, selling fake jewelry and conning people at fairs and bazaars with shell games, then he graduated to organizing gangs of "confidence men" who traveled the south, predominantly Texas and Colorado, bribing policemen and duping trusting souls at every stop. Smith gradually evolved from a quaint flim-flam man to a major con artist. He developed a vast array of underlings and opened gambling establishments filled with rigged games and "investment opportunities" that were run by fake mining and minerals experts.

Soapy Smith earned his nickname through a scam in which he would set up a stand on a corner and begin barking about the amazing soap he was selling. In order to entice buyers, he would wrap bars of soap as he spoke, and he made a great show of including money, sometimes $1 bills, sometimes $100 bills, in the packages he wrapped. He would then put the bars into a big basket, and then he would begin auctioning off the bars of soap. Every so often someone in the crowd would open a bar with money inside, and would whoop and holler and show off the money he'd "won." What people didn't know, however, was that Soapy had plants in the audience, and only these shills were lucky enough to buy the winning bars of soap. It was a very convincing scam.

Soapy utilized the "Prize Package Soap Sell" for over a decade. It helped him accrue three major empires of crime. The crimes of Soapy's organization became so well known that it was common for the soap gang to warn intended victims of the many swindlers roaming the city. In this manner the swindlers would gain the trust of their victims and lead them directly into their web of deception.

Another scam involved the display of "McGinty, The Petrified Man." For only a dime, the curious could line up to view a real petrified corpse. The scam took place as people waited in line to see poor McGinty, where they were fleeced with shell games, card games, and other rigged endeavors.

With the news of gold discovered in western Canada, the Klondike Gold Rush was on, and Soapy saw an opportunity. He headed to Skagway, where the stampeders began their journey in earnest, and set up a network of saloons dedicated to separating the prospectors from their money. In one scam, the Soap Gang offered prospectors the opportunity, for $5, to send a telegram anywhere in the world. Later, for $5, they could receive the inevitable "reply." The con lay in the fact that there was no ability to send or receive telegraphs in Skagway until years later.

Soapy was a con man, a really good one. He knew gullibility when he saw it, and he designed his businesses to take advantage of the trusting.

(Soapy Smith's family has built an impressive website about this king of con men: for more information, visit *www.SoapySmith.net*.)

The #1 Shady Character(s) of Modern Times: The Hunt Brothers

In the 1970s and 80s, the infamous Hunt brothers, enormously wealthy oil barons from Texas, effectively cornered the market in silver. Using billions in oil profits, they drove up the price for silver until they owned a substantial amount of the world's wealth in silver. But they didn't know when to stop. The Hunt brothers weren't just buying silver; they counted on a continued rise in price, so they were also buying futures. When Paul Volcker stepped in at the Federal Reserve and determined to get inflation under control, then raised interest rates, the excess liquidity in the market dried up and the price of silver began to fall. The Hunt brothers were cornered by their own futures bets; when the margin call came in, they couldn't make it, and were forced into bankruptcy. (We'll read more about the dastardly Hunt brothers later.)

A History of the Gold Standard

The issue of whether or not the United States could or should return to the gold standard is a source of some debate. In this section we will examine the definition, historical precedent, and the pros and cons of the gold standard.

There are several types of ways in which a country can adopt a gold standard. First, the *gold specie standard* is an economy in which actual gold coins are used in financial transactions. The *gold-exchange standard* is an economy where the metal coins and paper currencies in circulation are backed by gold reserves held by the government and are redeemable for gold bullion according to a guaranteed rate. A *qualified gold standard* is a variation whereby gold is held in reserve for a *portion* of every dollar in circulation. A *convertible gold standard* means that a nation's currency is tied to the currency of another nation that is on the gold standard.

First, a brief history of the gold standard:

The gold standard was first adopted in 1821, in Britain. Germany and France followed, then the United States, after making significant gold discoveries. The massive spending required by war meant the gold standard ended in 1914.

By 1928, the gold standard was re-established, but it was modified as a gold-exchange standard, which meant that most nations supplemented their gold reserves with U.S. dollars and British pounds (which were convertible into gold). This type of system is called a parasitic gold standard because two countries (or more) essentially bank of the gold reserves of one country.

The gold-exchange standard collapsed during the Great Depression, was re-established after World War II, then was finally abandoned by the United States in 1971 after dwindling gold supplies made the standard unfeasible.

A More Detailed History of the Gold Standard

If you really want to know more about the history of the gold standard and why it ultimately was abandoned, we'll go into more detail. Here we go:

Let's start in the 1870s, when the United States first adopted the gold standard. There was a completely free and unencumbered market for gold, and gold could be exported and imported without restriction. Paper dollars became officially redeemable in gold in January 1879.

A system of free coinage existed, which meant that anyone could take pure gold to a mint and have it minted into gold coins, receiving $20.67 for each ounce.

All this was codified into law by the Gold Standard Act of 1900. Under this act, the value of every dollar of paper money and of silver, nickel, and copper coins and of every dollar payable by bank check was equal to the value of a gold dollar—namely, equal to the value of 23.22 grains of pure gold coined into money. At this point, physical discoveries of gold around the world affected gold's value.

Things changed with the first world war. There wasn't enough gold to pay for the cost of that war, so the gold standard was abandoned. It was resumed after the war, abandoned during the Depression and again after the second world war, then, when it resumed, it was modified, since most nations could not afford to maintain a true gold standard.

The parasitic standard was a dangerous system, for if the principal nation's central bank was in trouble, so were all the depositor nations. In 1931 the gold standards of Austria, Germany, and Great Britain collapsed, the last dragging down several nations on the gold exchange standard with it. This was the beginning of the end of the gold standard in modern times.

Many British economists, notably J. M. Keynes, suspected that the monetary system was more vulnerable to disruption largely because of the inflexibility of the gold standard.

The Effects of Hoarding on a Gold Standard

In the United States the gold coin standard continued until 1933, when the public began to hoard gold.

Now, here's an event that lives in goldbug infamy:

On 6 March 1933, President Roosevelt declared a nationwide bank holiday for four days to stop heavy withdrawals and forbade banks to pay out gold or to export it. The public was panicking. Several banks had already closed. On 5 April, with Executive Order 6102, the president confiscated all gold coins and gold certificates of more than a hundred dollars, in exchange for other forms of currency. The government took in $300 million of gold coin and $470 million of gold certificates.

Executive Order 6102 made it illegal for individuals or corporations to own gold or gold certificates, but it did exempt the ownership or use of gold for industrial, professional, or artistic use, and it also allowed the possession of numismatic coin collections. This is important today because, as you'll see, many sellers of numismatic coins use this bit of history as a selling point, even though we are no longer on the gold standard, which makes the threat of confiscation highly unlikely.

Order 6102 did have the effect of stabilizing the currency. Citizens were paid $20.67 per ounce of gold that was turned in; the price of gold from the Treasury for international transactions was then raised to $35 an ounce. The resulting profit was used to fund the Exchange Stabilization Fund, which was established by the Gold Reserve Act of 1934.

Executive Order 6102 was revoked in August 1933, but private ownership of gold certificates was not legalized until 1964 (but they were still not redeemable in gold). In 1974,

President Gerald Ford signed a bill legalizing private ownership of gold coins, bars, and certificates, and in 1977 gold was again legalized for use in contracts (the so-called gold clause).

Only one person was prosecuted under Order 6102, and that prosecution was later ruled invalid on a technicality (the order was signed by the President and not by the Secretary of the Treasury, as required). Contrary to myth, contents of safety deposit boxes were not confiscated during the period of Executive Order 6102.

The Gold Reserve Act

With the Gold Reserve Act of 1934, the Unites States was moving away from a strict gold standard and was, in effect, introducing measures that allowed for more flexibility in the money supply.

This "qualified gold bullion standard" meant that only other countries could redeem dollars for gold (not individual citizens). Even then, the exchange rate had to be favorable. After France left gold as a standard in 1936, the qualified gold bullion standard in the United States was the only gold standard left in a world of managed currencies.

The system didn't work very well. The $35/oz. price greatly overvalued gold, stimulating gold mining all over the world and causing gold to pour into the United States. The "golden avalanche" aroused considerable criticism, yet still citizens were not allowed to redeem dollars for gold.

Keynes Opposes the Gold Standard

In 1936, Keynes's *General Theory of Employment, Interest and Money* proposed the idea of controlling the business cycle. The idea of a more managed economy was revolutionary. The idea that unemployment could be managed by slight increases in the money supply (inflation) made the cruelties of boom and bust cycles seem unnecessary.

Keynes's timing was perfect. With the costs of the Depression and the second world war making the gold standard impossible to maintain, Keynes offered an alternative. The appeal of a more managed economy was undeniable. The global gold standard had proven to be unsustainable. Instead, a new method of managing the world's economies was on the horizon.

The Creation of the IMF

After World War II a new international institution was created: the International Monetary Fund (IMF). The IMF was agreed to at a United Nations monetary and financial conference held at Bretton Woods, New Hampshire, in July 1944. Delegates from 44 nations agreed to the institution, and it went into effect in 1947.

The purpose of the IMF was to provide stability among national currencies, and at the same time to give devastated or debt-ridden nations the credit to reorganize their economies.

Dollar as Reserve Currency

The U.S. dollar was the reserve currency of the IMF. IMF countries could choose to redeem their currencies for dollars, which were still backed by gold. For about a decade dollars were much sought after. But as almost annual U.S. deficits produced a growing supply of dollars and increasing short-term liabilities in foreign banks, general concern mounted. Some of these dollars were the reserve base on which foreign nations expanded their own credit. The world had again, but on a grander scale, the parasitic gold-exchange standard it had had in the 1920s.

U.S. Treasury officials faced a great amount of pressure: the dollar's being a reserve currency imposed a heavy responsibility on the United States. Other countries complained: by running deficits and increasing its money supply, the United States was enlarging its reserves and, in effect, "exporting" U.S. inflation. But Asian wars, foreign aid, welfare, and space programs produced deficits and rising prices year after year.

A Run on Gold Begins

Possessing more dollars than they wanted and preferring gold, some nations—France in particular—demanded gold for dollars. U.S. gold reserves fell from $23 billion in December 1947 to $18 billion in 1960. Anxiety grew. When gold buying on the London gold market pushed the price of gold to $40 an ounce in October 1960, the leading central banks took steps to allay the anxiety, quietly feeding enough of their own gold into the London market to lower the price to the normal $35 and keep it there.

In an effort to preserve U.S. wealth, on 20 July 1962 President John F. Kennedy forbade Americans to own gold coins abroad after 1 January 1963. But federal deficits continued, short-term liabilities abroad reaching $28.8 billion by 31 December 1964, and gold reserves fell to $15.5 billion.

The Treasury took steps to discourage foreign creditors from exercising their right to demand gold for dollars. The banks felt it wise to cooperate with the Americans in saving the dollar, everyone's reserve currency. By late

1967, American gold reserves were less than $12 billion. In October 1969 Germany upvalued the mark again, and American gold reserves were officially reported at $10.4 billion. Foreign creditors grew alarmed. During the first half of 1971, U.S. short-term liabilities abroad shot up from $41 billion to $53 billion, and the demand for gold continued to rise.

The End of Bretton Woods

On 15 August 1971, after a run on U.S. gold reserves and a rapidly destabilizing dollar, President Richard M. Nixon suddenly announced that the U.S. Treasury would no longer redeem dollars in gold for any foreign treasury or central bank. This action, later referred to as "Nixon Shock," took the nation off the gold standard and shook reliance in the dollar as the world's reserve currency.

The dollar began a steep decline, and gold began to rise. In 1971 the dollar was devalued by almost 8 percent, and in 1972 the price of gold hit $70 an ounce.

A period of severe inflation followed the Nixon administration's decision to abandon the gold standard. Nevertheless, despite the economic turmoil of the 1970s, the United States did not return to the gold standard, choosing instead to allow the international currency markets to determine its value.

Floating Exchange Rates Begin

In 1976 the International Monetary Fund established a permanent system of floating exchange rates, a development that finally made the gold standard obsolete. The free market was used to determine the value of various international currencies. Consequently, as inflation weakened the U.S. dollar, the German mark and Japanese yen emerged as major rivals to the dollar in international currency markets.

After a period of instability, in the 1990s the U.S. dollar stabilized, and, by the end of the decade, it had regained a commanding position in international currency markets. The robust global economic growth of the 1980s and

1990s appeared to vindicate the decision to vacate the gold standard.

Even though the fiat dollar has injected an element of uncertainty, volatility, and skepticism into the market, it has also provided liquidity that some argue has allowed our monetary system to weather economic and political stresses, such as the 9/11 attacks and the fiscal meltdown of 2008, when credit markets froze amid rampant fraud and speculation in the housing market.

Key Dates in the Recent History of Gold

Some key dates in gold's trading history covering the period from the early 1970s through January 2012.

August 1971 – The dollar came off the gold standard. With some minor variations this had been in place since the Bretton Woods Agreement of 1944 and fixed the conversion rate for one Troy ounce of gold at $35.

August 1972 – The United States devalued the dollar to $38 per ounce of gold.

March 1973 – Most of the major countries adopted a floating exchange rate system.

May 1973 – The United States devalued the dollar again, to $42.22 per ounce.

January 1980 – Gold hits record high at $850 per ounce. Causes included high inflation because of strong oil prices, Soviet intervention in Afghanistan, and the impact of the Iranian revolution, which prompted investors to move into the safety of gold.

August 1999 – Gold fell to a low of $251.70 on concerns about central banks reducing gold bullion reserves, while, at the same time, mining companies were selling gold in forward markets to protect against falling prices.

October 1999 – Gold reached a two-year high at $338 after an agreement by 15 European central banks to limit the gold sales.

February 2003 – Gold reached a four-year high

on safe-haven buying in the run-up to conflict with Iraq.

December 2003 – January 2004 – Gold broke $400, reaching levels last traded in 1988. Investors started to buy gold as risk insurance for portfolios.

November 2005 – Gold rises above $500 for the first time since December 1987, when the spot hit $502.97.

April 11, 2006 – Gold reaches the next big level of $600, the highest since December 1980, with funds and investors pouring money into commodities on a weak dollar, firm oil prices and geopolitical worries.

May 12, 2006 – Gold prices peak at $730, the highest level since January 1980, with funds and investors pouring money into commodities on a weak dollar, firm oil prices and political tensions over Iran's nuclear ambitions.

June 14, 2006 – Gold falls 26 percent to $543 from its 26-year peak after investors and speculators went on a flurry of profit taking.

Nov 7, 2007 – Gold peaks at a 28-year high of $845.40 an ounce.
Jan 2, 2008 – Gold breaks above $850 for the first time since 1980.

August 22, 2011 – Gold hits record $1,901.70 in after-hours trading.

December 2011 – A price correction means gold falls to $1,531.

February 2012 – Gold is volatile, with dramatic price swings in both directions.

(Sources: GFMS, World Gold Council, Commodity Research Bureau, GoldPrice.org and Reuters database.)

Chapter 6: The Gold Standard Today, Government Debt, and Other Big Issues

A Return to the Gold Standard?

Whether or not the United States should return to the gold standard has become a topic recently addressed by some presidential candidates. Let's consider the pros and cons of the gold standard as opposed to fiat money, or paper dollars that are not backed by gold. These are the issues (in no particular order).

Under a Gold Standard, Currency Remains Stable

When dollars are backed by gold, inflation and deflation are minimized, but not entirely eliminated, because the actual physical amount of gold on the world market varies. Because currency cannot be printed without physical gold held in reserve to back it up, the threat of excessive paper currency (inflation) is virtually eliminated.

Government Debt and Deficit Spending Is Discouraged

Being on a gold standard discourages government debt and deficits; the government cannot float notes or speculative bonds since it would be prohibited from printing money to cover those effective loans.

Fiscal Discipline Is Ensured and Government Intervention Eliminated

Before the World War I and the Great Depression, it was generally assumed that there was no need for government intervention in the market. It was assumed that markets could self-correct. But another assumption was that there would be no need for significant government spending, or borrowing.

Following the tremendous borrowing that took place to finance the war, and the horrific struggles endured during the Depression, most economists revised their assumptions about the need for some flexibility and liquidity that could be pumped into the economy in times of crisis.

Why the Gold Standard Has Been Abandoned

Flexibility Is Key

One way to look at the issue of the gold standard is to compare it to the way in which private citizens run the typical household economy. For almost everyone except the extremely wealthy, taking out loans is the common approach to large purchases. Most people cannot afford to pay cash for a car or a house, so they get a loan from the bank and promise to pay interest on the loan, along with principal payments, until the loan is repaid. Without the flexibility of the loan mechanism, few would be able to afford these large purchases. The loan mechanism has the effect of raising the standard of living.

Similarly, the government sells bonds and Treasury bills when it needs to raise money. Those instruments are issued with the promise to repay them, along with interest, at some agreed-upon time in the future. This flexibility allows for large-scale purchases, or programs, that could not otherwise be funded.

The Money Supply Becomes Too Tight

If a country is on the gold standard, it loses the flexibility to print money to cover loans that have been issued. The result is an extremely tight money supply. If a country needed to raise money quickly (one example would be the funds that were needed in the immediate aftermath of Hurricane Katrina, or 9/11), then it would be required to either sell gold, or sell notes backed by the promise to repay in gold. Liquidity and flexibility would be severely restricted. (On a side note, a balanced budget amendment would provide the same type of limited flexibility; while there is undoubtedly a need to curb deficit spending in the United States, many fear that a balanced budget amendment would be too restrictive in times of emergency.)

Restricting government spending is not necessarily a bad thing, some would argue. But what it means is that, in times of financial stress, the government can do little to help. The government's ability to manage the economy would be restricted; a recession would be far more likely to spiral into depression. It also makes war prohibitively expensive.

In practical terms, under a gold standard, the Fed would no longer be able to reduce the money supply by raising interest rates in times of inflation, or increase the money supply by lowering interest rates in times of recession. In other words, the money supply would have to remain constant. (This is, in fact, why many advocate a return to the gold standard. It would enforce fiscal discipline, a balanced budget, and limit government intervention.)

From Barron's Banking Dictionary:

The main drawback [of the gold standard] is that it hinders the ability of a government to control the supply of money and it makes it difficult for a country to isolate itself from depressions or inflation in the economies of its major trading partners.
A country experiencing a large balance-of-payments deficit may thus find it impossible to properly address the situation without coming off the gold standard.

Limited Growth

The down side is that a fixed money supply, dependent on gold reserves, would limit economic growth. Many businesses would not get funded for lack of capital. Fluidity in the market would be severely restricted; many small businesses would fail, and other would never get the capital they need in order to get started. Unemployment would skyrocket without liquidity in the markets.

Large-scale projects that the United States embarks upon would become a thing of the past. Maintaining a large military would become onerous. Expensive projects such as interstate highways, bridges, dams, and airports could not get funded. Of course, notes and bills could still be issued, but, with the enforced guarantee that they would be repaid in currency backed by gold, the government could not afford to take the risk that, should the economy be in a slump at a later date, the gold would be unavailable.

The Price of Gold Is Uncertain

Gold has historically been subject to price fluctuation. The current trending upward in the price of gold is no hedge against the likelihood that a price correction will occur. In fact, a correction is even more likely.

The Value of the Dollar Is Relative

Is our economy weaker because we are not on the gold standard? No. The value of the dollar is always seen in relation to other world currencies. While the United States may be overextended, we are still a safe-haven for investors fleeing the instabilities of the euro zone, an inflationary China, and other world markets that are less stable than ours. Not being on the gold standard does not necessarily make our economy any weaker.

Practical Concerns

Practically, the United States could not unilaterally convert to a gold standard if the rest of the world didn't. If it did, every country that holds U.S. debt in the world could demand that the U.S. replace their dollars with gold.

The U.S. does not have enough gold, at current rates, to pay off the portion of its debt owed to foreign investors. For example, China, Japan and other countries own $3.2 trillion in U.S. Treasury debt, but there is only $223 billion (at $914 per ounce) total in gold reserves at Fort Knox, according to the Office of the Inspector General.

What this means is that, if the United States unilaterally returned to the gold standard, other countries could redeem dollars for gold until the U.S. coffers were empty. (Those who claim that gold could go to $10,000/oz. use this scenario as the basis for their calculation: if the United States divided the amount of gold we have in reserves by the dollars in circulation, then you arrive at approximately this figure. There are many problems with this scenario, but the biggest is the fact that the Unites States owns just a fraction of the world's available gold. We cannot unilaterally fix the price of a global commodity.)

The Issue of Fairness

What if the world went on the gold standard, and every currency of every country was backed by gold?

There is an inherent unfairness in choosing gold as a currency. Countries that had ample natural resources could simply mine their way into wealth. What this amounts to is digging gold out of the ground, melting it into coins or bars, then digging another big hole (a vault) and storing it back under ground. No inherent wealth or item or service of value has been generated. It is a very inefficient source of wealth.

Inherent Costs

Another practical concern is the physical cost of maintaining reserves. Storing, maintaining, protecting, and keeping track of the physical wealth of the United States would siphon billions of dollars a year out of the economy.

Finally, governments under the gold standard have shown a tendency to hoard gold instead of stimulating or aiding the business climate when needed.

Today, our currency is backed, not by gold, but by the "full faith and credit of the United States." We have never been late on a payment. We have never defaulted on a loan. (This is why the debt-ceiling debate in 2011 was so damaging to U.S. financial interests. Legislators who allowed even the suggestion of the idea that the United States would not pay its debt cast doubt on the fundamental integrity of the entire country and the strength of our financial institutions.)

What keeps gold bears cautious, however, or the reason some are still cautious about gold, is twofold. First, gold has historically been subject to price fluctuation. The current trending upward in the price of gold is no hedge against the likelihood that a price correction will occur. In fact, a correction is even more likely. Second, the value of the dollar is always seen in relation to other world currencies. So, while the Unites States may be overextended, we are still a safe-haven for investors fleeing the instabilities of the euro zone, China, and other world markets that are less stable than ours.

Today, the U.S. economy is an important partner in an integrated global economy. Central banks work closely together throughout the world to manage monetary policy. The ramifications of having the world's largest economy adopt an isolationist position and lose fiscal flexibility would be devastating to both domestic and global economies. Realistically, the United States could not adopt an isolationist economic stance, and abandon its ability to manage its economy using monetary policy, by returning to a gold standard without causing great harm.

The History of the Gold Standard and *The Wonderful Wizard of Oz*

Was the tale of *The Wizard of Oz* a populist allegory about departure from the gold standard, or just a story for children?

While there is no conclusive proof, an article in the 1964 *American Quarterly* by Henry

Littlefield posited an interesting interpretation: L. Frank Baum's *Wizard of Oz* can be read as an allegory about the late 19th century debate about whether or not to introduce silver into the monetary system (bimetallism). "Oz," the abbreviation for ounce, is the first hint, along with the yellow brick road representing gold, Dorothy's silver shoes (they weren't red until the movie version, when they were used to demonstrate the brilliance of Technicolor), and the Emerald City representing Washington, D.C. The allegory holds up with the tin man representing a worker dehumanized by industrialization, the scarecrow representing the farmers who were thought to be too dumb to comprehend the issue, and the lion, who was thought to represent William Jennings Bryan, a leader of the silverite movement. The Wicked Witches of the East (bankers) and West (railroad and oil barons) opposed the bimetallic system since it would have devalued gold and made their investments worth less. In the end, Dorothy returns home by clicking her silver heels together, which represents the fact that the solution (bimetallism) was there all the while.

The Question of Government Debt

Why Government Debt Is Not Necessarily a Terrible, Awful Thing

If a household continually spends more than it makes, the consequences can be dire. If a household has an annual income of $50,000 but spends $65,000, every year putting the balance on credit cards, then after a few years the debt will be insurmountable and the family will be forced into bankruptcy.

According to the website *Consumerism Commentary*, government debt is different from privately owned debt for several reasons:

-- The government can at any time, at its discretion, increase revenue. It's not popular, but raising taxes is an option. Households cannot similarly decree that their income increase.

-- The government can at any time, at its discretion, devalue its debt. Monetary policy comes into play. The Federal Reserve, working alongside the government, purchases government securities, increasing the money supply for banks and consumers. With more money available in the economy, people (mostly businesses) can afford to pay more, and prices increase, effectively decreasing the purchasing power of a dollar. This is a great position for people who owe money to be in, because the real value of what they owe decreases. (Households, on the other hand, have no control over the money supply and therefore cannot manipulate the real value of their debt.)

-- Deficit spending helps spur the economy. Throughout the 20th century, the government was more frequently in a budget deficit than in a budget surplus. The ability for the government to spend freely helped this country become the rich economic powerhouse it is today. With the federal government taking up the slack by investing in the economy during periods in which businesses were hesitant to invest, the country continued prospering — particularly the middle class. Periods of deficit spending were followed by periods of surplus, but for the most part, deficit spending is linked to this country's growth.

Over time, extreme deficit spending will cause problems, of course. Interest on debt is one of the largest national expenses, and having to continually pay for expenses already incurred is not a wise use of resources. Even through the devaluation of currency, it's unlikely this problem will ever be tackled. Unlike a household, though, government can keep postponing the consequences. The best a household can do would be to declare bankruptcy. Other nations have taken this approach to have an opportunity to restructure their debt, but it's unlikely for this tactic to be used the United States in the near future.

What is more likely is that "quantitative easing," or QE, which is Federal Reserve lingo for infusing more dollars into the system by buying up government-issued bonds, will be used to add "liquidity" to the system and dilute the value of the dollar. Some inflation will result, which will reduce the real costs of government debt. Flush with cash, companies feel the confidence to start hiring, tax revenues go up, and the system cycles from recession to growth.

What this means for potential gold buyers is that we are currently in a state of instability and flux, which is usually a good time to buy gold. The basic, fundamental reason to buy gold, remember, is as a *store of wealth*. If inflation is anticipated, then owning gold is a way to protect your money.

For example, if you have $10,000 in a coffee can under the sink and quantitative easing begins, then the value of that money will slowly begin to erode. After a few years it will effectively be worth less. But if you buy $10,000 worth of gold, the value is (relatively) locked in. If inflation sets in, the value of the gold will track with inflation, and after a few years, if you want to sell that gold, the price will have risen along with everything else.

If only it were so easy.

On the other hand, gold is a commodity that is influenced by many factors.

In an unstable global environment, when the euro zone is in crisis and China is struggling to control inflation, the dollar is seen as a reserve currency, a last bastion of strength. As the dollar rallies, the price of gold typically weakens. The dollar may have problems, but it is still the strongest currency in the world.

Another factor: in inflationary times, dollars spent on other items of value, such as real estate or stock in strong companies, will earn substantial interest. Gold, which doesn't earn interest, can be seen as less appealing.

As we move on to the more practical aspects of buying, selling, or holding gold, keep in mind that these are the reasons why diversification of any portfolio is vital. The value of gold will rise and fall. It may go sky high; it may plummet. It will never be worth *nothing*, but the bubble may burst. Having *some* money in gold is a good idea. How much? Read more before you decide.

Chapter 7: Sorting Through the Maze

You've seen the ads. Gold appears to be a relatively easy thing to sell: so many people are doing it.

Watch the ads for companies selling gold. Listen to the sales pitches. They tend to have a few things in common. First, they appeal on a primal level. Piles of gold are displayed: glittering, shiny, tangible. Second, gold sellers appeal to a desire for safety. The world is uncertain, but gold is solid and dependable. Finally, sellers tend to evoke a sense of fear. Buy "before it's too late." For some the fear component is relatively tame: "Buy because the price of gold will go up." For others, the fear tactics are heavy-handed: "Buy to protect you and your family from ruin and devastation."

By now you have a pretty good feel for the market and a basic understanding of why gold is a strong hard asset to have in any portfolio. But let's look a little closer at some specifics.

An honest examination of companies selling gold shows that some of the most prominent companies, such as Goldline, are also the very companies that are under investigation for consumer fraud.

Goldline, in fact, has been investigated by the SEC. One report, by investment broker Peter Schiff, notes that Goldline has a past of ripping off customers and overcharging. In the example Schiff gives, Goldline sold a French Rooster for $402 (the buyback of that same coin by Goldline was $260). Meanwhile, other dealers were selling that same coin for $250.

There are basically two types of gold that gold dealers sell: bullion, and numismatic coins. Bullion tends to be low-priced and competitive. As we've seen, some sellers will invoke Executive Order 6102 and try to convince you that numismatic coins are the only truly safe bet. But that is also where the most profit is made.

Comparing Prices

GoldPrice.org is a particularly valuable resource when it comes to checking the day's spot price and comparing real-time bullion prices from various dealers.

One site that seems to consistently offer value is BostonBullion.com.

Kitco.com offers a daily rundown, often technical, of what is happening in the gold market. TheStreet.com is another useful source. One feature on the site is Alix Steel's "Daily Gold Guide," a two- to three-minute video interview of traders and brokers who are carefully tracking the day-to-day movements of gold.

Gold Is Your Friend, but Not Your *Best* Friend

Gold has a place in any well-diversified portfolio. Ideally, it is purchased when gold is reasonably priced: not necessarily at a historical low, but not at an all-time high, either.

Historically, gold tootles along in the $200-500 range. From 1976-1980, during a time of high inflation and political turmoil in the Soviet Union and in Iran, gold temporarily skyrocketed to $850 (or $2,079 when adjusted for inflation). Like a bullet shot into the sky, the price fell back to earth, and by 1999 the price was $251/oz.

In 2008, gold began a steady march upward. In September 2011 the price briefly touched $1,900, then it quickly readjusted and settled in at the $1,600-1,800 range.

The point is that gold is currently behaving erratically. No one has a crystal ball, and most of those who predict that gold is on a never-ending upward trajectory have either 1) not studied history, or 2) are in the business of selling gold.

Ways to Invest Wisely in Gold

The business of buying, selling, or holding gold can be confusing. Three rules of thumb to keep in mind:

- Resist high-pressure or fear-based sales tactics.
- Learn the market before you buy. Comparison shop. Due your due diligence.
- Be aware of hidden costs.

If you are interested in gold as a hedge against uncertain times, against inflation, or simply for portfolio diversification, then you are in the market for gold coins or bullion. Bullion is basically gold in its simplest form: bars or coins with no added value based on design, age, or appearance. (This is gold in its purest form as opposed to coins with numismatic value, or value based on condition, age, or scarcity.) Unless you want to become a rare coin collector, you want to buy bullion.

What's the Best Way To Buy Bullion?

Do your homework, but know that the second you get online and order an investment kit, the phone will start ringing, and on the other line will be a sales associate (or "investment advisor") who wants to sell you gold. Right then. And, if you decline, they will keep calling. (I ordered an investment kit from Goldline and was called more than 10 times before I convinced them to stop calling.)

A more hassle-free approach is to comparison shop online and know what you want before you place that call. Most online dealers do not accept credit cards for bullion, although some, like Blanchard, accept credit cards for numismatic coins. For bullion, they complete the transaction verbally, lock in your price, then you send in a cashier's check or money order.

Storage Fees and Premiums

Most gold purveyors offer access to a secured vault where, for a fee, your gold can be securely stored. Blanchard, for example, uses a privately-owned secured vault called The

Security Center (www.securitycenter.com), which is a former Fed gold vault in New Orleans that provides all the secure whistles and bells: double-keyed locks, code numbers, and handwriting verification, for example. But renting this type of security isn't cheap: vaults range in size from 2" x 5" x 24 and start at $166/year, and go up to large lockers that rent for close to $700/year.

Keeping in mind that you are not earning interest or dividends on that wealth, the price of storing gold can quickly eat into its worth as an investment vehicle.

A more cost-effective approach would be a safe-deposit box at your local bank, which usually range in cost from $25-50/year. You'll still pay fees to ship and insure your purchase, but that will be a one-time fee, as opposed to a yearly cost. (If you're worried that the government will freeze all bank assets, buy a fire-proof safe and store it in your attic.)

Finally, be aware of the premiums that are charged. To buy gold coins, premium costs usually range from 2-11%. Numismatic coins typically carry a much higher premium than bullion.

Understand the Downside

Jon Nadler, senior analyst at *Kitco.com*, has been warning of a fast and furious exit by traders and hedge funds, which could pummel the gold price. While "rabid gold bug forums and doomsday-oriented newsletters where defiance rules the day and denial is the favorite flavor of the moment" are still common, says Nadler, there are plenty of analysts who think that gold could be primed for another correction and could see a drop by as much as 33 percent off the September 2011 high.

Understand What You're Buying

According to Michael Kosares, author of *The ABCs of Gold Investing*, "The biggest trap investors fall into is buying a gold investment that bears little or no relationship to his or her objectives. Take safe-haven investors, for example. That group makes up 90% of our clientele [at *USAGold.com*]. Most often the safe-haven investor simply wants to add gold coins to his or her portfolio mix, but too often this same investor ends up instead with a leveraged (financed) gold position or a handful of exotic rare coins (often costing five or six figures). These have little to do with safe-haven investing, and most investors would be well served to avoid them -- except as a sideline."

Gold and the Tax Man

The IRS considers gold and other precious metals to be "collectible," which means that, when you sell, if you make a profit, that profit is heavily taxed—up to 35 percent.

Under federal tax law, "collectibles" include:

- Works of art
- Rugs and antiques
- Metals and gems
- Stamps and coins
- Alcoholic beverages (vintage wines and rare liquors)

"Normally, when you sell a capital asset you've owned for more than one year, your tax rate is capped at 15 percent. But when you sell a collectible, tax law caps your maximum rate on long-term capital gains at 28 percent, not 15 percent. In other words, on a $100,000 gain (lucky you!), that means you don't pay $15,000 to Uncle Sam, you pay $28,000 -- an extra $13,000," says MSN Money analyst Jeff Schnepper.

"If you hold the asset for less than a year, it gets worse. Your gain becomes a short-term gain, and it's taxed at regular income tax rates. That means a rate of as much as 35 percent."

Changes to the Tax Code

Section 9006 of the Patient Protection and Affordable Care Act will amend the Internal Revenue Code to expand the scope of Form 1099. Currently, 1099 forms are used to track and report the miscellaneous income associated with services rendered by independent contractors or self-employed individuals, according to reports by Strategic Property Exchange, LLC.

As of Jan. 1, 2012, Form 1099s are used to report to the Internal Revenue Service the purchases of all goods and services by small businesses and self-employed people that exceed $600 during a calendar year. Precious metals such as coins and bullion fall into this category, and coin dealers have been among those most rankled by the change.

This provision, intended to mine what the IRS deems a vast reservoir of uncollected income tax, was included in the health care legislation ostensibly as a way to pay for it. The tax code tweak is expected to raise $17 billion over the next 10 years, according to the Joint Committee on Taxation.

Tax Reporting Requirements

Effective January 2012, all sales of precious metals of any kind in excess of $600 are reported to the IRS on Form 1099B. There are, however, some exceptions. A more thorough examination of current tax policies on the sale of gold and other precious metals can be found at *www.spe1031.com*.

Gifting Gold

Currently, gifts are nontaxable up to $13,000 per recipient per year and can be given to any number of people, providing a convenient and legal avenue to bypass the otherwise inevitable inheritance and/or estate taxes on the gifted portion of a person's wealth. Gift-splitting provides even more power to transfer wealth. If you are married, you and your spouse can separately give tax-free gifts up to $13,000 each to the same recipients, equating to a total annual non-taxable transfer of $26,000 per recipient. Separate gifts can be given to as many recipients as desired. Furthermore, gifting through the Uniform Transfers to Minors Act (UTMA) may provide additional tax benefits while allowing you (or another responsible adult) to serve in a custodial capacity for the benefit of a minor recipient. (As always on matters of taxation and tax planning, including various gifting strategies, please consult with your tax advisor.)

Precious Metals Exchange

Buying or selling precious metals is a reportable tax event, and the taxes can be steep (in the range of 25-35 percent). However, there is a way to legally avoid this type of tax through a precious-metals exchange. This type of transaction must be done very carefully in order to meet tax code requirements. For more information on avoiding taxes through precious-metals exchanges visit *www.spe1031.com.*

Gold in Relation to the Stock Market

In his book *Basic Economics*, Thomas Sowell argued that, in the long-term, gold does not hold its value compared to stocks and bonds:

> *To take an extreme example, while a dollar invested in bonds in 1801 would be worth nearly a thousand dollars by 1998, a dollar invested in stocks that same year would be worth more than half a million dollars. All this is in real terms, taking inflation into account. Meanwhile, a dollar invested in gold in 1801 would by 1998 be worth just 78 cents.*

Gold does not earn interest or pay dividends, so investors buy gold to store wealth when they anticipate times of economic or political instability. In the end, buying gold comes down to two factors: a desire to protect existing value, and an expectation of dire economic or political circumstances. (As we've seen, that value is not protected fully. The price of gold can still go down. But there is some inherent value, so some measure of value is certain.)

Historically speaking (over the past 30 years), gold is relatively low when it is priced in the $300-500 range per ounce. It is in the medium range at $500-900, and it is high at anything over $900. While the current market is considerably higher, current bears see a bottom of $1,300, and the current parlor game of pundits amounts to this: "Gold 2012: $1,000 or $2,000?" Clearly, buying any commodity on the high side is risky, at best.

These are conservative figures, but they can serve as a guide when trying to decide whether or not to buy gold. The current price of gold, which is over $1,700 and peaks and dives in the $1,600-1,900 range, is a historical anomaly, similar in appearance to the bubble of the early 1980s. (The question, of course, is whether this is a bubble or an accurate reflection of global uncertainties.)

Gold and Inflation

According to economist and *Wall Street Journal* contributor Jeff Opdyke, in theory gold should track with inflation. The traditional assumption is that gold and inflation rise and fall together; in inflationary times, in theory investors would seek the safe haven of the precious metal. As the value of the dollar declines, gold remains more stable. Conversely, when inflation is very low, the dollar is stronger, so gold becomes less appealing and gold prices fall.

But what has happened over the past 30 years is actually different: gold has continued to climb while inflation is at a record low. In essence, gold is not "behaving correctly," which could be a sign that a herd mentality is factoring in and a price correction is likely.

It boils down to this: For investors convinced U.S. lawmakers and central bankers will successfully manage the budgetary woes and the massive unfunded liabilities of Social Security and Medicare, then gold is overvalued in the long term. Righting America's national balance sheet would explicitly raise the dollar's value as investors with money abroad move assets into a more-sound U.S. economy. The selling of euro, yen, and pounds would push the dollar higher—and gold lower.

If, however, you worry the U.S. balance sheet is irreparably damaged, then gold currently reflects the likelihood that a weak-dollar trend still has years to run as the United States struggles with its financial mess. Investors—and consumers—looking to preserve their purchasing power will gravitate toward gold, since its quantity isn't easily manipulated.

Financial instability in global markets is another factor; until the euro zone figures out a way to either salvage or scrap the euro, the uncertainties there spill over into other global markets. China and India are emerging markets for gold as well, for both personal and investment purposes. Uncertainties in global markets can mean good news for holders of U.S. stocks, dollars, and gold. (The dollar, in particular, which is a favorite whipping boy for the pro-gold crowd, is still a strong bet when compared to other global currencies.)

A Safe Haven

"Gold is still a safe haven," says Jeff Clark, Casey Research's Senior Precious Metals analyst, "but it is a tradable asset and people buy gold for different reasons," from inflation, deflation, debt worries, panic to economic calamity. On any given day one of these factors becomes more prevalent, argues Clark.

Recent market trends indicate more traders buying long positions on gold, as well as many cashing in to take advantage of short-term gains. "On one hand, that means more committed long buying. On the other, the positions might be the first to be liquidated if traders have to raise cash fast. The tug-of-war translates into one thing: volatility," says Clark.

Clark believes that gold needs time to breathe. "The run up that we had [in the fall of 2011] was dramatic enough that it's not surprising that it will take some time for the gold price to consolidate before it makes new highs," which he thinks might be during 2012.

Longer term, Clark is still bullish on gold. Currently, approximately 10 percent of federal revenue now goes to debt but, according to the Congressional Budget Office, that number could triple. "That is a dramatic amount and that is going to have an impact on the purchasing power of the dollar, and that is the kind of environment that one wants to hold gold in."

The fact that gold is increasingly considered "sticky," which means that investors are buying gold with no intention of selling in the short term, is another factor that makes gold appealing long-term.

The Big Question

So, then, the big question lingers. Should you buy, sell, or hold gold—right now?

Clearly, investing in gold is murky, at best. No one has a crystal ball, and the market for gold is not behaving in any way like it has in the past, so trends upward or downward mean little. What this means for the average investor is that gold is not foolproof, it is not a guaranteed source of increased wealth, but it can add a measure of stability to a portfolio.

Sellers of gold will urge potential clients to invest up to 30 percent of their savings in gold. More conservative investment advisors advocate a 10-percent holding. The bottom line is that investing in gold is not a surefire bet. The price of gold may go up, but it may plummet, too. Some think gold will continue to skyrocket; others think the bubble is about to burst. The takeaway is to invest in gold as a counterbalance to stocks and bonds, and only invest money that you do not need in the short term.

Gold as a Store of Wealth

As we've seen, in general terms, gold represents a store of wealth (without growth), whereas stocks are valued as a potential return on value.

The importance of taking a longer, educated view cannot be overestimated. Know what you're buying, and be realistic about probable returns. Understand the risks, and know how and where the pitfalls are. Ask questions. Understand where dealers make their money. For all the risks, portfolio diversification remains the single best reason to invest in gold. When other asset classes tank, gold will be fine. If you're buying gold not out of fear, or out of a desire to get rich quick, but as a means to add depth to your holdings, then your reasoning is sound.

Finally, keep in mind that the market to buy and sell gold is filled, FILLED, with hucksters, shysters, and thieves who overcharge for the gold itself then run up exorbitant fees in storage, insurance, and maintenance fees. Do your homework. Compare companies and extra fees. Know that if you are going to wade into the market for gold, it is filled with sharks.

There will always be someone out there telling you that gold is going to go to $5,000, $6,000, or even $10,000 an ounce. But now you have the knowledge to decide for yourself whether or not this is indeed a likely scenario. And if the dollar does become so destabilized and hyperinflation arrives, as it would if an ounce of gold really cost $10,000, then Fareed Zakaria might be right: it might be smarter to invest in canned beans.

Resources

BlanchardOnline.com

Coin and Precious Metal Values 2010 by Jim Kingsland

CoinResource.com

Connected: 24 Hours in the Global Economy by Daniel Altman

FactCheck.org

The Federal Reserve by Preston Martin and Lita Epstein

Financial Armageddon by Michael J. Panzner

Goldline International

GoldSilver.com

GoldVox.com

Guide to Investing in Gold & Silver by Michael Maloney

Money.com

The New Paradigm for Financial Markets by George Soros

TheStreet.com

World Gold Council

Amount of debt held for foreign creditors: U.S. Treasury Major Foreign Holdings of U.S. Debt; Office of Inspector General, Audit Report, November 2007

Chandler, Lester Vernon. *American Monetary Policy, 1928–1941.* New York: Harper & Row, 1971.

De Cecco, Marcello. *The International Gold Standard: Money and Empire.* New York: St. Martin's Press, 1984.

Eichengreen, Barry J. *Golden Fetters: The Gold Standard and the Great Depression, 1919–1939.* New York: Oxford University Press, 1992.

Gallarotti, Giulio M. *The Anatomy of an International Monetary Regime: The Classical Gold Standard, 1880–1914.* New York: Oxford University Press, 1995.

Kemmerer, Edwin Walter. *Gold and the Gold Standard: The Story of Gold Money, Past, Present and Future.* New York: McGraw-Hill, 1944.

Mehrling, Perry G. *The Money Interest and the Public Interest: American Monetary Thought, 1920–1970.* Cambridge, Mass.: Harvard University Press, 1997.

Ritter, Gretchen. *Goldbugs and Greenbacks: The Antimonopoly-Tradition and the Politics of Finance, 1865–1896.* New York: Cambridge University Press, 1997.

Schwartz, Anna, and Michael D. Bordo, eds. *A Retrospective on the Classical Gold Standard, 1821–1931.* National Bureau of Economic Research. Chicago: University of Chicago Press, 1984.

The ABCs of Gold Investing by Michael Kosares.

Index

A

B

C

I

J

K

L

M

N

W

Z

www.ingramcontent.com/pod-product-compliance
Lightning Source LLC
Chambersburg PA
CBHW051507170526
45166CB00001B/421